Special Praise

"I can't wait to give *Hard to Love* to both male and female clients involved in difficult relationships! Nowinski adroitly and sensitively integrates theory, clinical examples, and pragmatic strategies for both therapists and clients in this well-organized and engagingly written book. His sensitivity to gender issues and an under-recognized clientele is a huge contribution to the field of mental health."

Barbara F. Okun, PhD
Professor, Northeastern University

"In *Hard to Love*, Dr. Nowinski explains a complex issue affecting men in a way that is at once easy to understand, interesting to read, and even, at times, entertaining. This book encourages men to be honest about themselves while simultaneously offering hope and help not only to the men, themselves, but to the people who love them."

Kristine Tsetsi
Journalist and Author of Pretty Much True

"Dr. Nowinski's knack for making complex clinical concepts clear comes through in his new book, *Hard to Love*. He remains a master of interweaving vignettes and cases to illustrate the clinical conditions that fly below the radar of many clinicians. His stories inject life into the textbook criteria and give the reader a new perspective on the subject. As with breast cancer in men and heart disease in women, many men with borderline personality suffer needlessly due to misdiagnoses. What's more, Dr. Nowinski reminds us that persons with borderline personality don't suffer alone. Everyone around a person with borderline personality disorder seems to suffer, and they will continue to suffer until someone identifies the core problem.

"Thank you, Dr. Nowinski, for a fresh perspective that will resonate with clinicians and people from all walks of life. Yes, men with borderline personality are difficult to love, but they are not impossible to love. I find it difficult not to love this book and nearly impossible to put down once you pick it up!"

Robert Doyle, MA, DDS, MD
Assistant Medical Director,
McLean Child and Adolescent Inpatient Unit
Harvard Medical School

Co-author with Joseph Nowinski of Almost Alcoholic

HARD TO LOVE

HARD
TO LOVE

Understanding and Overcoming Male
Borderline Personality Disorder

JOSEPH NOWINSKI

CENTRAL RECOVERY PRESS
LAS VEGAS

Central Recovery Press (CRP) is committed to publishing exceptional materials addressing addiction treatment, recovery, and behavioral healthcare topics, including original and quality books, audio/visual communications, and web-based new media. Through a diverse selection of titles, we seek to contribute a broad range of unique resources for professionals, recovering individuals and their families, and the general public.

For more information, visit www.centralrecoverypress.com.

Publisher: Central Recovery Press
3321 N. Buffalo Drive
Las Vegas, NV 89129

19 18 17 16 15 14   1 2 3 4 5

ISBN: 978-1-937612-57-3 (trade paper)
       978-1-937612-58-0 (e-book)

This book contains general information about male borderline personality disorder. The information is not medical advice, and should not be treated as such. Central Recovery Press makes no representations or warranties in relation to the medical information in this book; this book is not an alternative to medical advice from your doctor or other professional healthcare provider. If you have any specific questions about any medical matter you should consult your doctor or other professional healthcare provider. If you think you or someone close to you may be suffering from any medical condition, you should seek immediate medical attention. You should never delay seeking medical advice, disregard medical advice, or discontinue medical treatment because of information in this or any book.

Central Recovery Press books represent the experiences of their authors only. Every effort has been made to ensure that events, institutions, and statistics presented in our books as facts are accurate and up-to-date.

To protect their privacy, the names of some of the people, places, and institutions in this book have been changed.

Cover design and interior design and layout by Sara Streifel, Think Creative Design.

For Gregory and Rebecca
with love

AUTHOR'S NOTE: The term borderline disorder was coined by psychiatrist Adolph Stern in 1938 to describe a group of symptoms that did not fall into either category of mental illness used at that time: neurosis or psychosis. Stern thought the symptoms exhibited by certain patients fell into the "border" between the two categories. The term "borderline" grew in usage among psychiatrists and psychoanalysts, until, in time, they began to consider the "Borderline Disorder" as a mood (or affective) disorder, rather than a type of schizophrenia (a thought disorder).

Today, the diagnosis of Borderline Personality Disorder (BPD) refers to people who have a negative self-image and who have a pattern of difficulty sustaining relationships. As a result they can have difficulty controlling their emotions and can be self-destructive. BPD can vary from mild to severe.

In this text, I refer to MBPD, or Male Borderline Personality Disorder, as well as simply BPD (Borderline Personality Disorder). The two terms refer to the same constellation of causes, symptoms, and behaviors. However, while BPD is often accurately diagnosed and treated in women, the correct diagnosis, as well as appropriate treatment, is too frequently overlooked in men. That is what this book aims to address.

TABLE OF CONTENTS

PART ONE: UNDERSTANDING BPD IN MEN

PART TWO: SOLUTIONS FOR MBPD MEN (AND THOSE WHO LOVE THEM)

FOREWORD

Creating and maintaining a long-lasting intimate relationship is no easy task, and poses challenges for most of us. Even for those who were blessed with ample supplies of love, attention, security, etc. from their childhood caregivers, having a healthy and happy intimate bond requires tremendous fortitude and perseverance, plus a commitment to conscious and deliberate self-awareness.

No doubt, for those who did not receive adequate supplies of the necessary ingredients early on in life, the challenge can be daunting. Imagine how hard it would be if you not only didn't get many of the "goodies," but you also received a bunch of the "baddies," that is, neglect, abandonment, or abuse? Definitely not an easy task. Plus, to make matters even more difficult, many males are taught that they need to be as tough as nails and don't—nor should they—need the "soft" and "feminine" forms of nurturance that are reserved for a few lucky ones, girls.

For years, the field of psychology has been heavily saturated with attention and focus on women and the well-being of their relationships, particularly in terms of how to make their intimate bonds strong and healthy, as if the male gender's situation didn't matter. Tons of attention went toward understanding and diagnosing insecure and emotionally unstable women, both through the world of professional counseling and in the world of self-help. However, the male gender was seriously short-changed.

Well, men, too, can suffer from low self-esteem, insecurity, and enormous self-doubt that can result in serious emotional instability. It can reach the extreme wherein these states define all of a man's behavior and ultimately compromise the stability of his intimate relationships. And, sadly, because we've tended to stereotype men as "the tough ones," we have often missed the boat on understanding and appreciating the complexity of a man's inner world. Hence, we haven't even begun to provide guidance for men and their loved ones on how to help them overcome their experiences of deep pain from fear of abandonment and rejection, which underlie these insecurities. This is not a condition where you can tell a guy to "take two aspirin and call me in the morning." Rather, this condition, known as Borderline Personality Disorder (BPD), requires serious attention and an in-depth method of treatment. Plus, since many men still experience a negative stigma when it comes to seeking help for emotional issues, they are prone to deny their issues and often fail to seek or accept help. So what are these men and those who love them to do?

Many women I have known and worked with professionally have had the experience of dating a man who had initially presented himself with many endearing qualities and who at first seemed terrific. However, very quickly into the relationship, the women sense that something is off. For example, he may need to know their whereabouts all the time. He may freak out if his calls are not returned immediately. He may be subject to sudden and severe mood swings.

Until now there has been little to no literature available to explain what I am now certain is what Dr. Joseph Nowinski describes as the Male Borderline Personality Disorder (MBPD)— which he aptly describes in *Hard to Love*.

Fortunately, Dr. Nowinski's book offers us an easy-to-read, highly informative, and insightful guide for men with Borderline Personality Disorder and for their intimate partners. Using real-life examples coupled with a direct yet compassionate tone,

Dr. Nowinski guides the reader through a deep understanding of MBPD followed by a multidimensional solution. He illuminates such issues as how to deal with "free-floating" anxiety and insecurity. He teaches how to build self-acceptance, healthy boundaries, and resilience in both love and life. This is a truly comprehensive approach to understanding and overcoming this disorder.

Thank you, Dr. Nowinski, for writing such a much-needed work. May it help its readers end their emotional suffering and finally be able to see the light of hope and healing.

Debra Mandel, PhD
Psychologist and author of
Don't Call Me a Drama Queen!

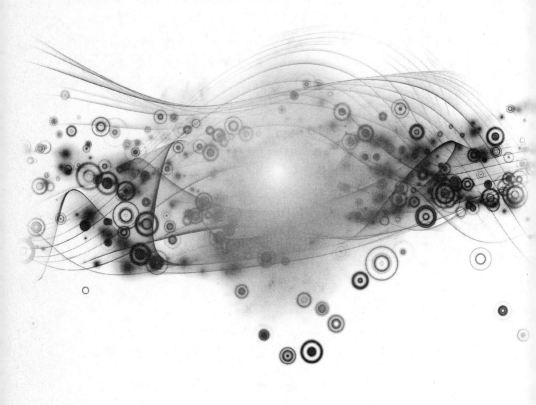

INTRODUCTION

Ever since the film *Fatal Attraction*, starring Glenn Close and Michael Douglas, captured the attention of moviegoers around the world, the concept of Borderline Personality Disorder (BPD) has become part of public consciousness. It is a diagnosis that has been used to refer overwhelmingly to those women who

- Have had ongoing problems making relationships work. Typically these women fall in love quickly and intensely, but their relationships are marred by unrealistic expectations and resultant conflict.

- Tend to see the world in black-and-white terms. In other words, you are either their best friend or their worst enemy.

- Demand attention. Sometimes they do this by being flirtatious; alternatively they may get attention by hurting themselves or threatening to.

- Are emotionally intense and unstable. They can come on strong sexually, but their anger can be equally intense, and they can sink into deep states of depression and hopelessness. Consequently, they can be alternately needy and rejecting.

- Cope with uncomfortable emotions through the use of alcohol and/or other drugs. Anger, anxiety, jealousy, self-hatred, depression, and boredom are only some of the emotions that the person with BPD tries to anesthetize with medication or drinking, often placing herself at risk of an overdose.

Until now the idea that men may also suffer from BPD—perhaps even in equal numbers to women—has received scant attention. There is very little written about BPD in men in the professional literature, and even less research. Treatment centers for BPD rarely admit a male patient. However, experts in the field acknowledge that this condition does exist. As Rex Crowdy, MD of the National Institute of Mental Health points out, the hallmarks of BPD, in particular the inability to manage inner feelings and to succeed in relationships, are just as common in the male population as they are among women. Yet men rarely receive that diagnosis, much less treatment for it. In addition, because men and women differ in what they mean by intimacy, their attitude toward anger, the basis on which they build self-esteem, and so on, the solutions for BPD in men and women also differ.

Hard to Love takes a fresh look at the concept of Borderline Personality Disorder and how that diagnosis may apply to as many men as women. Rather than framing it as a simple category—something one either is, or isn't, period—we will look at BPD as a personality and temperament style that exists on a spectrum.

As this book goes to print, the American Psychiatric Association has just published the first revision in fifteen years of its *Diagnostic and Statistical Manual of Mental Disorders,* or *DSM. DSM-5,* as this edition is called, attempts to clarify the definition of a "personality disorder." The category of BPD is retained in *DSM-5,* but also organizes the behaviors associated with it into two areas. Specifically, in order to qualify for a diagnosis of Borderline Personality Disorder, an individual must show significant impairment in the following two areas of personality functioning:

- Self: The individual has an essentially negative view of him- or herself.

- Interpersonal: The individual has a distorted view of others and difficulty in close relationships.

As you read further, you will see that Male Borderline Personality Disorder, as described here, matches those criteria very well. In addition, the view taken in *DSM-5* is enlightened in that it does not view a personality disorder as a simple category, that is, something one has or doesn't have. Rather, it acknowledges that personality disorders, including BPD, can vary from mild to severe. That is the point of view taken here as well.

One end of the BPD spectrum is anchored by what could be called "normal occasional male insecurity." This is the state that describes the overwhelming majority of "normal" men. It means that even the most psychologically healthy individual can have occasion to experience self-doubt, to experience intense emotional states, and to experience conflict or unhappiness in his relationships.

At the other end of this spectrum is full-blown Borderline Personality Disorder. In between these two anchor points is a large spectrum on which men's personalities and temperaments can vary greatly. It is only those men whose personalities and temperaments place them at the extreme end of the spectrum who truly have a mental illness for which they require expert help if they hope to ever experience personal satisfaction, inner peace, or a satisfying long-term relationship. Those who fall in the middle range—who show some of the signs of BPD but in a less severe form—are the men who are "hard to love." It is impossible to define precisely how many of these men are out there, but judging by the accounts of those who love them, there are many of them.

Hard to Love seeks to help two groups of people. One is composed of those men who suffer from BPD to one degree or another, but who are unaware that this is in fact the cause of their living problems. Many will have been misdiagnosed, for example, as antisocial or as having a substance abuse or anger management problem. As a result, any treatment they may have received will likely have been only partially successful, if at all. These men need a clearer understanding of

- Why they are struggling with BPD.
- What they can do to mitigate the symptoms of BPD so they can stop the suffering and lead more fulfilling lives.

The second group this book seeks to help is those who are in relationships with men who have BPD. What these readers need to know includes

- How to avoid unintentionally making BPD worse.
- Ways to facilitate and reinforce positive change in the BPD man in one's life.

This book is divided into two parts. Part One will focus on understanding Male Borderline Personality Disorder. It will include case vignettes and will answer such questions as

- Why has BPD in men been overlooked?
- What happens to men with BPD that's different from what happens to women with BPD?
- What are symptoms of BPD in men?

Part Two focuses on solutions for Male Borderline Personality Disorder. Again, it is aimed at two audiences: men with BPD and those who are in relationships with them.

While some readers may find it useful to engage the help of a therapist when tackling the issues described in the book, many (especially those men whose personality and temperament places them somewhere in the middle of the BPD spectrum) will be able to make use of the solutions that are offered on their own.

PART ONE

UNDERSTANDING BPD IN MEN

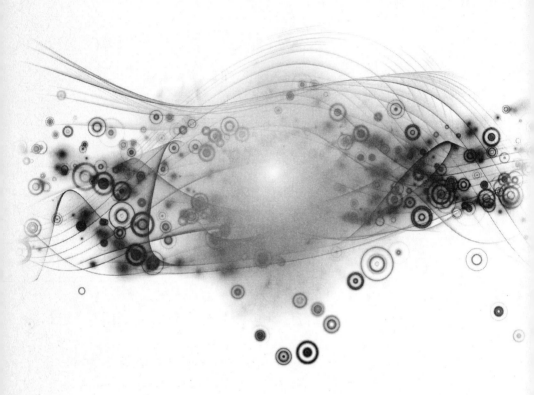

CHAPTER ONE

Men Who Are Hard to Love

Paul and Meg met in a bar when they were both in their mid-twenties. Meg rarely visited bars, in fact, she rarely dated, but she had been persuaded by some friends to go celebrate one of their birthdays. Paul had also been there with friends, and the two groups somehow gravitated to one another, eventually pairing off in a casual sort of way. Paul did not come on strong to Meg (which would have immediately turned her off), but before he left he did ask if it would be okay if he called her some time. She was skeptical, but gave him her number, and was pleasantly surprised when he called three days later, asking if she'd care to meet for coffee. Again, this low-key approach is what appealed to Meg.

Meg had been raised in a suburban middle-class family and had a younger brother and two younger sisters. Her father had been a teacher and made enough money to enable Meg's mother to work part-time at the local library while devoting the lion's share of her time to parenting and keeping house. Theirs was, Meg said, "the all-American family, at least when you looked at us from the outside."

Meg was bright and did well in school. She also enjoyed active play, and was more interested in building things and climbing trees than in traditional "girls'" pursuits like playing house or skipping rope. She was, unfortunately, also the victim of her father's occasional fondling hands and his tendency to be a voyeur. "I remember being angry that my parents would not allow us kids to have locks on our bedroom doors," Meg said. "That meant that I had to be constantly on guard for my father walking into my room, which I shared with my next youngest sister Joann. He was most likely to barge on in right after I took a shower, so I became very sure from an early age to always have some clothing on. The couple of times I complained he'd get all huffy and act like I was being ridiculous."

Meg believed that her mother never suspected that her father was a voyeur, much less that he'd tried groping his daughter on several occasions. Meg coped with the groping in two ways: by keeping her distance and also by "dressing down." "I had the largest collection of baggy jeans and sweatshirts you've ever seen!" she told me with a laugh, adding "It fit my tomboy personality."

"But it could also serve as camouflage, don't you think?" I suggested. Meg nodded.

Meg knew that Joann shared her experiences and concerns, though to a lesser degree, and they both believed that both their brother Tim and their youngest sister, Eliza, for whatever reason, had not drawn their father's interest. "We didn't talk about it much," Meg explained, "It was as if we both just knew on some level that our father was sleazy and we worked around it. I think Joann ended up having more trouble with it, though, because she became an alcoholic and then married a man I thought was a real loser. They got divorced, and she's in recovery now, but it seems to me she's still attracted to men who just use her because she makes a good salary as a nurse."

Meg, who was thirty-four at the time of our meeting, had gone to college part-time, but did not finish. Instead, six months after she met Paul she moved out of her house and in with him. It was the only impulsive thing she'd ever done, and she admitted that it had been totally out of character for the shy, cautious person she'd always been. But Paul appealed to her. He had a steady blue-collar job, was a hard worker, and shared her goals, which tended more toward raising a family than pursuing a career. Also, Meg could tell from occasional comments he would make that the idea of her being more educated than he was made Paul uncomfortable. So Meg dropped out of college and enrolled instead in a training program in a vocational school and became a machinist—one of the few females to work in that trade. And that had the added advantage, she said with a smile, of being a convenient way for her to continue "camouflaging" her body.

Meg and Paul married and had two children, a son and a daughter whom she described, with evident delight, as "my angels." They were healthy, did well in school, and enjoyed sports and swimming in the town lake during the summer. Meg was concerned about a couple of things, however, beginning with Paul's drinking.

Despite her low-key nature and the fact that she had not dated much before meeting Paul, Meg admitted that when she did go out with friends, she sometimes drank to excess. Then, after she and Paul got together they eventually fell into a pattern of having a couple of beers pretty much every night together— and sometimes more on the weekend. But she'd put those days behind her as soon as she got pregnant with her first child. Now she would have a beer or two on Saturday and/or Sunday, always with Paul. He, on the other hand, had continued to drink daily. He also smoked pot on the weekends. "He drinks either three or four beers, or else most of a bottle of wine, every night," Meg explained, "and if he gets into one of his moods he drinks more than that. Sometimes I'm not sure if the drinking causes him to get into a mood, or if it's the mood that makes him drink."

What Meg meant by Paul's "moods" was his tendency to sink into a severe state of depression, or else flare up with intense anger, with seemingly little provocation. He was, she said, extremely thin-skinned, and could take offense at things that others might consider trivial. For example, if he came home and felt "ignored" by her, when she was actually just busy taking care of the children, he might storm off in a huff. Drinking always made that situation worse. "If he's had more than three beers and gets into a mood, then we can't communicate at all. He just sulks or gets mean," Meg explained. "We both work full-time as well as raising two kids. It's like Paul is almost competing with them for my attention. I do try to pay attention to him, but there are times when I'm distracted or tired. He doesn't seem to understand that."

Here are a few examples of other issues that Meg was concerned about. From her perspective these issues clouded their relationship and, over time, were creating what she called a "distance" between her and Paul.

- Paul occasionally would complain that after Meg got pregnant he "lost his drinking buddy." Indeed, after they began to live together and up until Meg got pregnant she did drink almost as much as Paul did, and she also sometimes smoked pot with him on weekends. When Paul complained about losing his "drinking buddy," he would get sullen, and nothing Meg could say would lift him out of that sullen funk.

- On a few occasions when Meg tried to talk to Paul about his drinking—because she was concerned about how it was affecting his health and what it was modeling for the children—he would fly into a rage. At these times he would accuse Meg of thinking she was "too good for him." Then he'd mutter something about how she was probably looking for someone to replace him.

• Over time Paul had turned sour on virtually every friendship he had. From his perspective, Meg explained, people were always letting Paul down. "And he holds a grudge like you wouldn't believe!" she added. As a result, their circle of friends was extremely small, and their social life extremely limited.

• Paul's attitude toward friends extended to his work relationships, where he regarded most of his coworkers as lazy and his bosses as incompetent. He was not only extremely critical of them, but of people in general. He was inclined, for example, to blow up when frustrated about how someone in the car ahead of him was driving.

• Paul was very concerned that Meg dressed in ways that he would call "provocative." They had a limited social life, but even if they were going to a family function he would accuse her of "dressing sexy" so as to attract attention. He would also accuse her of flirting with his friends. According to Meg, however, "I don't own a single 'sexy' outfit! Just ask my friends."

• Whenever he was in one of his "funks," Paul would make disparaging comments about himself. "If he's trying to do some little repair job around the house I can hear him muttering words like 'stupid' to himself. And again, he often says that he thinks I will eventually 'dump' him for someone else."

Once, after they returned home from a gathering with friends, Paul again accused Meg of flirting with a man who at the time was Paul's best friend. Meg said she'd had a few drinks that night, admitted that it was only at times like those that she could allow her "feminine" side to show "even a little bit." But she denied that she'd been intentionally flirtatious. As she'd told me, she learned from an early age to keep that part of herself under wraps. I was inclined to believe that she was sincere about this.

Despite the fact that Paul was aware of Meg's history with her father, including the fact that she disliked flirtatiousness in other women and had never done anything that could make Paul distrust her, a fight nevertheless ensued between her and Paul, which she could not de-escalate. Then Paul pushed Meg. She stumbled backwards and fell to the floor. The racket woke the children, who emerged from their bedrooms in tears. Paul then proceeded to stomp around the house, upending a chair and further frightening the kids. Then he stormed out of the house, hopped into his truck, and sped off. At that point, fearing for what might happen if Paul returned in the same mood, Meg called her best friend, Jill, hastily dressed the children, and took them to spend the night with her friend.

Paul figured out where Meg and the children had gone as soon as he returned home to find his house empty. He called Jill's house and asked to speak to Meg. When she got on the phone he apologized profusely. He also agreed, albeit reluctantly, to see a counselor with her.

Paul suffers from Male Borderline Personality Disorder or MBPD for short. Like the vast majority of men with this disorder, he has not been diagnosed as such. Instead, the counselor he met with (only twice) gave him a "diagnosis" of alcohol abuse and also said that Paul needed to work on anger management. And though this may be objectively true—Paul did have a drinking problem and his behavior at times was aggressive—this would not be of much help in understanding Paul's behavior or changing it. And changing it would definitely be in Paul's interest as well as Meg's and their children's.

Paul

Though you could say that Meg's childhood was not exactly a bed of roses, Paul had it just as bad if not worse. His father had abandoned him and his mother when Paul was three and Paul never saw the man again. His mother, who was an alcoholic, subsequently married and divorced two alcoholics, both of whom were hostile and abusive to Paul. She'd had another son by Paul's first stepfather, and this boy was the recipient of whatever limited ability to provide love and nurturance that man had been capable of.

Paul's mother, meanwhile, seemed to have decidedly divided loyalties. Sometimes, Paul said, she would defend him when she thought he was being treated unfairly; at other times she would stand back and do nothing. Similarly, she could be affectionate with Paul at times, but usually only when they were alone together.

After Paul's second stepfather passed away, and after Meg quickly cut way back on her drinking, Paul turned to his mother, and she became what Meg described as "his new drinking buddy." Paul would visit his mother once or twice a week on his way home from work. Sometimes he would bring take-out food and they would sit around, eat, and drink beer. Paul would have had several drinks in him by the time he got home.

Meg felt that Paul had "mixed feelings" about his mother, given his upbringing, but that in some respects she was the only person he'd ever been close to. "And that includes me," she added with a sigh. Paul's mother died—of cirrhosis—when Paul's first child—his son Ethan—was a year old.

So, you might ask, given his personality and temperament, why would Meg be interested in Paul to begin with, and why would she stay with him? Indeed, men like Paul are not easy to love. But despite their obvious flaws, men like Paul are not one-dimensional. When asked to talk about what attracted her to Paul, and why she stayed, here is what Meg had to say:

- "First off, I liked Paul from the first time we met because I could tell that he was not just out to get me into bed. He seemed very respectful—never tried to grope me. Even when I'd had a few drinks he did not push himself on me. That was very important to me. It made me feel safe with him."

- "Paul is actually a very sensitive man. I know he can be very critical, but he's as critical of himself as he is of anyone else. He can be very good with the kids when he isn't drinking, and he enjoys playing with them or just watching TV with them."

- "I know that Paul is very jealous of me—thinks I'm smarter than him and that I'll eventually dump him. But he's also got skills. I don't know whether he just doesn't realize it, or he just doesn't value the skills he has. He built a play house for the kids. It took him two months, and it's a work of art—or should I say a labor of love? He's also a great cook when he's motivated to do it."

Is Paul *hard to love*? Yes, definitely. Is Paul *unlovable*? Not according to Meg. Sure, they had their problems—maybe serious ones. But as Meg pointed out to me, she didn't know anyone who had a perfect marriage. She didn't have any friends, she said, who she'd readily trade places with. She and Paul had two lovely children, and Paul was a steady worker who rarely missed a day of work. Though he occasionally spent money in ways she didn't think they could afford, such as an above-ground pool for the kids, he was not personally extravagant. She could typically expect Paul to get into one of his "moods" once or twice a week, but at other times there was relative peace in their house. Did she feel like she had to walk on eggshells around Paul? Yes, to an extent, but she felt that she was more or less aware of what could send him into a tailspin of depression or an explosion of anger. A little extra attention from her made daily activities go more smoothly between them.

Meg felt that staying together was her best alternative. So why did she come to see me? Because, although she had decided to stick with her marriage, on another level Meg knew that it could be better. Also, she knew that the one incident in which Paul had pushed her could not be repeated, both for her own self-respect and to spare her children from believing that such behavior in a marriage was acceptable.

It's safe to say that there are many men like Paul out there, and an equal number of women, like Meg, who want to make a relationship with a man like him work. These are the men and women for whom this book is written.

What will you learn here? You will learn, first, why men with MBPD are typically misdiagnosed and misunderstood. This is important because, as in Paul's case, it most often leads to a dead end. For example, simply telling Paul that he should do something about his drinking, or attributing his explosive outbursts or bouts of depression solely to his drinking, falls short of understanding the personality and temperament that contribute to both. Of course Paul may need to address his drinking, his temper, and his episodes of depression, but that is best done in the context of helping him (and Meg) to understand the context in which these occur (which is his MBPD) and what he can do to manage it.

Based on an understanding of MBPD, we can move on, in Part Two, to looking at a number of solutions these men (and those who love them) can pursue in order to "tame the beast" that troubles them on a deeper level. Facing those inner demons then sets the stage for men like Paul to lead more satisfying, less frustrating lives, and for those who love them to be able to share in those lives.

CHAPTER TWO

Beginnings: The Myth of the Tough Boy

As psychologists (and virtually all parents) have long known, children show definite sex differences and preferences when it comes to behavior, including play and risk-taking. And although research into the field of gender differences is opening up new thinking all the time, it is generally the case that from early childhood, most boys are more interested in rough-and-tumble play, and most girls are interested in more inwardly focused play. Boys are more likely to climb trees and have skinned knees, and girls more likely to favor imaginative, relationship-focused play. Boys are more likely to be fascinated with dragons, girls with horses. And though many boys are drawn to video and computer games based on combat and survival, most girls are not. There are exceptions, of course, but these generalizations are largely sound.

Behavior versus Personality

Behavioral sex differences like those just described appear to be the basis on which our society stereotypes boys' and girls' personalities. In other words, we've been inclined to see these *outer* differences as indicators of *inner* differences. These latter stereotypes, however, are not only generally inaccurate, worse, they can be downright dangerous. The specific stereotype I'm speaking of is the one that goes like this: *girls are sensitive, boys are tough.* Or, as the old rhyme goes:

> *"What are little boys made of?*
>
> *Snips and snails, and puppy dog tails*
>
> *That's what little boys are made of!*
>
> *What are little girls made of?*
>
> *Sugar and spice and everything nice*
>
> *That's what little girls are made of!"*

Again, the implication is clear: boys are *tough*, inside and out; girls are *sensitive*, inside and out. **Not true!**

If anything, research suggests that boys, despite their preference for rough-and-tumble play and their attraction to risk, may actually be more emotionally vulnerable and less resilient in the face of trauma than girls. We will look at this issue more closely later on, but for starters consider the following facts:

- The prevalence of alcohol abuse among men is almost three times as high as it is among women. People don't just drink for fun; they also drink as a means of coping. They drink because they believe it helps relieve anxiety or depression. This is especially true among people whose drinking—like

Paul's as discussed in the previous chapter—falls outside of what you could call "normal social drinking."

- Almost four times as many males as females die by suicide. People don't kill themselves if they are happy and psychologically resilient. So if we men are so tough, why do more of us resort to suicide?

- The incidence of "conduct disorders" is twice as high among boys as it is among girls. These disorders are typically associated with difficulty dealing with emotions. Boys are thought to be emotionally resilient, but in fact, they are just as emotional as girls; however, the myth of the "tough boy" may be what prevents boys from feeling their emotions and expressing them in anything other than the limited socially acceptable ways for boys: fighting and roughhousing. After all, "boys will be boys" and "boys don't cry."

This thinking that boys are emotionally thick-skinned is one reason why boys can grow to become men with MBPD.

Attachment

Attachment is one of the key developmental tasks facing a young child—basically, a child between the ages of birth to five. It happens to be one of those rare psychological terms that is actually self-explanatory. Beginning at or soon after birth, children become "attached" to others. They also can become "attached" to places and to objects.

The most common first attachment is to the mother, who is usually the first person to hold, cuddle, and nurture the newborn. However, attachment is not limited to the mother, but can include the infant's father, as well as others who provide comfort and nurturance and who interact with the infant on a regular basis. The key to attachment appears to be nurturance and comfort. Attachments form the "home base" where a child feels safe and from which he or she will venture forth to discover and learn.

Abandonment, abuse, and rejection hold the potential to seriously undermine or disrupt attachments that are either being formed or that have already been formed. The same is true for parents whose behavior reflects ambivalence toward a child. In Paul's case, described in the first chapter, his father left him at an early age and his mother remarried twice, each time to an abusive alcoholic. And she, at least according to Paul as well as his wife Meg, was not a model of consistent nurturance or comfort, perhaps as a consequence of her own alcoholism. She acted with ambivalence toward her son, protecting and nurturing him at some times, while abandoning or rejecting him at others. This parenting style breeds the kind of insecurity that is common among people with BPD. The sexual stereotypes just described, however, can make us "color blind" (or "gender blind") so that we fail to see this cause-and-effect chain in boys as much as we are open to seeing it in girls.

When attachment becomes problematic the result can be long-term insecurity. That insecurity can manifest in several ways. First and foremost it can lead to what is called "free-floating anxiety." This is a form of anxiety that more or less hovers over a person. They can tell you that they are anxious, but they typically can't say what they are anxious about. You can also think of insecurity as a nagging feeling that the people you love won't necessarily be there for you if you need them. Insecurity leads a person to be overly vigilant for any signs of rejection. In turn, the insecure person is slow to forgive a perceived rejection.

Insecurity can also be manifested in a fear of exploring the world, trying new activities, or taking risks. Along with this is a need for constant reassurance and a tendency to be clingy— these are all clearly evident in men with BPD.

Finally, abandonment, abuse, and rejection lead to self-hatred. Why? To put it simply, children are by their nature trusting and loving. Moreover, their formative experiences take place almost exclusively in the context of the parent-child relationship. Therefore, if they are neglected, rejected, or abused they are inclined to conclude that they are "bad" or "inferior," as opposed to blaming their parent or caregiver for that. From their point of view, what else could explain their abuse or rejection, other than that they are somehow unlovable? Why else would their parent act with ambivalence toward them? This too was evident in Paul as an adult, for example when he would call himself "stupid" if he made a mistake, and when he would accuse his wife of feeling "superior."

If their initial attachments are successful, children will be able to form additional attachments to significant others later on, with peers as well as with other influential adults in their lives, such as babysitters and day-care workers and, later, with teachers and coaches. I've met many people who can attest to how a teacher, a coach, a sibling, or other relative stepped up to the plate during their formative years and became that emotional anchor they needed.

I believe, as do many psychologists, that healthy attachments in childhood set the stage for satisfying, committed adult relationships that are not poisoned by insecurity. They lead to a positive self-image instead of one that is marred by self-hatred. Unhealthy or failed attachment, in contrast, sets the stage for precisely the insecurity and self-hatred that are the hallmarks of MBPD.

Not Just People

Children also become attached to objects, such as stuffed animals and blankets. They use these things as supplemental attachment objects. These items represent additional sources of comfort and companionship, particularly when human attachment figures are not readily available. All parents can attest to the various kinds of objects that their children become attached to, anything from a toy dragon to a stuffed kangaroo. Some families have heartwarming stories of their children's attachment objects that were eventually packed up to accompany the "child" to college.

Adults, not just children, can also form attachments. Indeed, insecure people may be more inclined to do so than those who are relatively secure. This may include you, or someone you love.

What about Boys?

Our thinking about attachment may not be the same when it comes to boys, whom we are inclined to stereotype as rugged compared to girls. One mother, for example, expressed concern because, after she and her husband separated, their four-year-old son Tyler became attached to a doll named Sparkle.

Sparkle had long, dark brown, curly hair that glittered in the light—hence the name. This mother had originally gotten the doll for her older daughter, who was more or less indifferent to it and expressed no objections when Tyler appropriated it.

It was obvious that Sparkle was a source of comfort to Tyler, and that it was no coincidence that this new attachment followed closely on the heels of his father moving out of the house.

Tyler carried Sparkle with him constantly and would not go to sleep at night unless Sparkle was tucked in at his side. His mother's concern was that Tyler might be ridiculed by other children for carrying a doll. This was a real possibility, especially if Tyler decided that he wanted to bring Sparkle with him to the day-care center his mother dropped him off at every morning on her way to work. To avoid that possibility I suggested that Sparkle be tucked into bed each morning, where she would spend the day waiting for Tyler to return.

Tyler maintained his attachment to Sparkle until he was six. Then, for some reason known only to Tyler, Sparkle was retired to a drawer beneath his bed. Tyler then began sleeping instead with a rubber snake and one or more stuffed dogs, which he'd begun collecting.

Tyler's father kept in regular contact with him after the separation. Still, Tyler (more so than his sister) would cry inconsolably on occasion, saying that he missed his father. He also had occasional nightmares, the only cure for which was to sleep in his mother's bed (with Sparkle at his side). His mother expressed surprise at this, saying that (for reasons she could not put into words) she'd expected her daughter to have the harder time. When I suggested that the reason might be an underlying assumption that boys were "tougher" than girls she thought for a moment, then nodded.

Because his parents accepted Tyler's anxiety, and did what they could to comfort him, and also because Tyler was able to maintain his attachment to his father, his story had a happy ending. He was able to weather the storm created by his parents' divorce. When it was time to start school he did so without difficulty and had none of the social or academic problems that are common in one of four children of divorce.

Young children like Tyler, of course, cannot be counted on to put their insecurity into words. Instead, one has to "read" it in their behavior. In turn, there are two ways to respond to their behavior. The right way is the way Tyler's parents responded: with understanding and tolerance. The wrong way is to try to ignore the behaviors or try to talk boys out of them.

"Don't feel that way!" will not be sufficient to make insecurity go away. Even worse are efforts to shame boys out of their insecurity. Unfortunately, because they buy into the myth of the tough boy, parents sometimes try to get boys to "tough it out" or "man up." It would have been a mistake, for example, to try to persuade (or force) Tyler to give up Sparkle, or to insist that he stay in his own bed after having a nightmare. It would have been much worse, of course, if Tyler had lost his relationship with his father as a result of the divorce. Fortunately, that was not the case.

Taking Stock

Many of the symptoms associated with problems of attachment can be seen in adult men with BPD. The problem is that, as adults, they do not usually "connect the dots" and see how their insecurity, self-hatred, or anxiety may be rooted in the stereotype that they ought to be tough; therefore, they resist seeing such a connection. They may well buy into this stereotype themselves. Like Paul, they may get huffy and defensive if someone even suggests that they may be "insecure."

The good news is that it is possible to work on overcoming the effects, such as those just described. However, that healing cannot begin until a man is aware of how his temperament and personality as an adult relate to his experiences as a child.

Early Memories

Early memories often reveal those to whom we were attached as children, as well as to the strength and security of those attachments. Here is an example:

Michael's parents had divorced when he was six. His father, an engineer, was bitter. He ended up taking a job with an oil company in another country, remarried, and rarely returned to the states to see his son. When Michael came for counseling—the result of escalating conflict with his wife, combined with periodic bouts of severe depression that recently included an accidental overdose of sleeping medication—he said he did not remember much about his father. But according to his mother, he explained, he'd initially cried virtually every night at bedtime after his father left.

Later on Michael developed temper tantrums, and eventually a reputation for being someone who could fly off the handle. The depression, in contrast, did not begin to set in until he was an adult.

Despite his emotional ups and downs Michael did well in school, went to college, and became an accountant. He said that he had few friends, and inwardly had always been an anxious person who distrusted others and was self-critical. His relationships with women had also not gone smoothly. He'd been told, more than once, that he was "smothering." From his point of view, though, the women he'd chosen to get close to were always letting him down. During his college years two of them had ended up cheating on him before breaking off the relationship. He saw no connection, however, between these women's behavior and his tendency to be smothering and possessive. This problem existed now, as well, with his wife complaining that Michael was too controlling in the marriage, both of her and their children. He countered that he was a good provider and a faithful husband who was simply trying to instill good values in his children.

In counseling Michael was asked to think, between sessions, about any early memories he had of his father and to write them down. Here is what he came up with:

- A vague image of him leaning up against his father on the family room couch, watching a cartoon show and laughing together.

- Reading at night before bed. Michael's father would lie beside him and they would go through their regular ritual that included reading a story and then giving each other a special, "secret" handshake.

- Going with his father to a nearby park and being pushed on the swings. Michael also vaguely remembered screaming in excitement when he felt he was being pushed too high, and his father then catching the swing and stopping it.

Michael could not figure out the significance of any of these early memories. Indeed, he had not thought about any of these attachments from his earlier life for many years. His therapist, however, suggested a couple of ways in which they could be relevant. The memories suggested, for example, that Michael's father had been a major source of comfort for him before he left. He read bedtime stories to Michael, which is not only comforting to young children but cements the attachment between parent and child. Finally, Michael's father was a source of fun (taking him to the park and pushing him on the swings) as well as security (being able to stop the swing whenever Michael got anxious).

It was pretty evident, then, that Michael's father had actually played an important role in his life during his early years, and that the father-son bond had been strong. Then, after the divorce, Dad (and the father-son attachment) was suddenly gone. Viewed from the perspective of young Michael, he had not only been loved, but also abandoned by his father. This lost attachment would later be reflected in Michael's difficulty getting close to others. He still had few friends, and was notably distrustful as well as jealous. His wife said the word "smothering" seemed right.

Despite his success Michael could be dreadfully self-critical. And, he had a temper, but could also fall into deep states of depression. Even the slightest criticism would send him into an emotional tailspin. These traits were all part of his borderline personality.

The following exercise is designed to help you take stock and reflect on your early experiences of attachment.

Your Early Memories

It can be productive to take some time, as Michael was asked to do, to reflect on your earliest memories with each of your parents. Here are a couple of ground rules:

- Don't rush this process. Your initial response may well be that you don't have many (or any) memories of your childhood. That may be the case, but if you allow this idea to "incubate" for a couple of weeks you will most likely find some memories emerging. Some of these may come to you suddenly, "out of the blue," so to speak, when you least expect it. Some may even come to you when you are asleep.

- Write your memories down in a journal or notebook of some kind. This can be helpful as these memories can easily fade out of consciousness again.

- Be looking out in particular for memories, like Michael's, of interactions you may have had with your father and mother, as well as any other adults you lived with.

- What emotional tone is associated with each of your memories? Do these memories evoke feelings of warmth and comfort? Conversely, do they evoke anxiety? Anger?

- As you look over your memories, do you get an impression that one of your parents may have had mixed feelings (ambivalence) about you? Which one? How was this ambivalence reflected in his or her behavior?

- Who do you think you were most attached to as a child? Were any of these attachments broken, for example by divorce or abandonment?

Places

In addition to people and objects, children can also form attachments to places. Think about this:

- When you were a child, did your family vacation in the same place year after year?

- Was there a space in your home where you felt comfortable and especially liked spending time?

- Did you like to arrange your bedroom (or your part of it) in any particular way?

- Would you be upset if anyone changed the way you'd arranged objects in your life?

The above are all examples of attachments to places. One man I counseled, Tom, spoke fondly of a tree house he and an older brother had built as children. Tom had a strong attachment to his brother, as well as to his mother. Their father had been a gambling addict who'd abandoned the family when Tom was three, apparently as a way of fleeing his debts. Tom not only spent time with his brother in that tree house, which was complete with a shingled roof and screening to keep out insects, but also used it as a refuge. On hot summer nights he often slept in the tree house alone, reading by the light of a lantern until he fell asleep.

As adults we sometimes think of this form of attachment as nostalgia: as a simple longing for days gone by. But these attachments are real, not just wistful thinking. They contribute to that sense of safety and stability that children rely on as a "home base" from which to venture forth and explore the world. Frequent disruptions in these attachments provoke deep anxiety of the "free-floating" variety described earlier.

As you were growing up, did you form attachments to places, as well as people and objects? Were these attachments stable, or were they often broken? This frequently happens, for example, to boys who grew up in a series of foster homes, and it often occurs with little notice.

SUMMING UP

Although problems of attachment may not be the sole cause of BPD in men, I believe it is certain that they play a large role. Our tendency to view boys as tough and rugged—not just physically, but emotionally—can set them up to develop the traits and temperaments associated with MBPD. They in turn can internalize that stereotype and expect themselves to be impervious to traumatic experiences such as abandonment, abuse, and rejection. As they evolve into men these boys may well be blind to the connection between their earlier experiences and their adult personalities and problems of living.

CHAPTER THREE

MBPD: Misunderstood, Mistreated, Men

Imagine that you are a therapist and I refer a client to you using the following brief description:

> Dear Dr. Jones:
>
> Thank you for agreeing to meet with Chris, who is thirty years old. Chris currently works full-time as a graphic designer while also taking graduate courses evenings and weekends toward an advanced degree, and hopes to eventually secure a teaching position in a community college.
>
> Chris reports a history of severe difficulty in relationships, specifically feeling "let down" and "taken advantage of" on

several occasions. Chris also reports some trouble controlling emotions and apparently can "swing" from intense depression to intense anger rather quickly. This also often happens in the context of relationship conflict. As a teen, Chris reports having engaged in some minor "cutting" behavior when stressed, though this stopped a few years ago. Since then, however, Chris admits to drinking heavily when under stress or when feeling depressed. Chris was prescribed an antidepressant one year ago and though the medication is taken as prescribed, Chris does not feel that it has helped much. Accordingly, I am referring Chris for counseling with you.

What is your first impression: Is "Chris," as described in the above "referral":

• A thirty-year-old *woman*, or

• A thirty-year-old *man*?

Take a moment to read the following:

I have long wondered what was wrong with me. I have intense emotional swings where I can go from being angry to almost giddy in a flash, or else fall into a deep depression. I can't seem to tell what triggers these mood swings, though they sometimes seem to control my life and cause a lot of trouble for me in relationships.

I am sensitive and creative, and I've always worn my feelings on my sleeve, as they say. I cry easily, both in joy and sadness, and also have these weird episodes of anger. I've been told I am thin-skinned and often take words or feelings personally that others say aren't intended that way.

What do you think? Is this a woman or a man describing him- or herself?

The overwhelming majority of people who read these statements tend to believe they were penned by a woman who is describing herself. In fact, they are the statements made by a man.

In the case of the imaginary referral above, this same bias emerged when a group of fifty-two professionals working in a mental health agency in California were asked to make a provisional diagnosis of a patient—identified as either male or female—based on a description of his or her symptoms. These professionals were unable to accurately diagnose the presence of Borderline Personality Disorder in men despite the fact that the symptoms were exactly the same in the two descriptions. In other words, these clinicians, as experienced and well trained as they may have been, were essentially "color blind" when it came to seeing BPD in men versus women.

What is the source of this bias, and why is it important?

Buying into Sexual Stereotypes: Tomboys and Sissies

The bias that leads people to think that the previous examples describe a woman instead of a man have their roots in the sexual stereotypes that were the subject of the last chapter, namely the idea that boys (and men) are inherently rugged and resilient, whereas girls (and women) are inherently delicate and sensitive. One doesn't have to look far to find visual and written reflections of these stereotypes. They are conjured, for example, in the "reality" television series about men who make a living catching alligators with their bare hands from a rowboat, or by mining in the harshest reaches of the earth, or by shouting abuse at employees of their restaurant kitchens. We see this type in television ads for trucks and in movie characters such as Iron Man or The Incredible Hulk (who has a stereotypically "male" way of expressing anger)— "Hulk smash!" Even the socially prominent CEO in his custom suit lords it over his workers, and relishes snapping out, "You're fired!" without a trace of sensitivity. These men, society seems to say, are "real men."

Traditionally, female characters were not allowed to exhibit behaviors like the above and still be considered "real women." Instead, they were portrayed as the "hooker with the heart of gold" as in *Pretty Woman,* or the "manic pixie dream girl," as bubbly, eccentric, and elusive as Holly Golightly in *Breakfast at Tiffany's,* or as the nurturing and motherly Mrs. Weasley of *Harry Potter* fame.

Our culture is beginning, though, to accept more active, competitive, and "tough" female characters. In recent years images of strong and resilient women have increasingly appeared. Consider, for instance, Ellen Ripley in the *Alien* films, Lisbeth Salander in the book/film *The Girl with the Dragon Tattoo,* or the youthful heroine Katniss Everdeen in the book/film *Hunger Games.* Similarly, women's competitive sports are increasingly evident on television. Although it is safe to say that even today, women athletes are presented as less aggressive than, say, male football players. Women basketball and tennis players are just as competitive as their male counterparts, but are still frequently the subject of attention as much for their appearance and personalities as for their aggressiveness.

Generally, though, women today seem to have a larger variety of models to follow, and more types of ways to be a "real woman." But men, by and large, still have only the "silent" or "violent" stereotypes on which to model themselves.

Is there a kernel of truth in sexual stereotypes? Perhaps. Statistically, men do commit crimes of violence much more frequently than women do. And men do occupy professions that require sheer physical strength in significantly larger numbers than women do. On the other hand, when a recent candidate for the US presidency voiced the opinion that women ought not to be placed in direct combat duty positions in the military he was roundly criticized. In reality, women do occupy combat positions in the military, and women can act as aggressively as men in that position. So attitudes, at least, are changing. That said, there remains a good deal of deep-seated cultural bias about the way men and women should be.

And both men and women are inclined to buy into stereotypes about how they ought to be. Evidence of this attitude can be found in how our culture reacts to those whose behavior and temperament differ from these stereotypical expectations. As mentioned earlier, the term "tomboy" has long been used to refer to girls who, unlike so-called "princesses," or "girly girls," are inclined to wear rough-and-tumble clothing and engage in rough-and-tumble activities. Tomboys, like their biological boy counterparts, are more likely to be interested in climbing trees or playing contact sports than experimenting with make-up or playing with dolls. Tomboys, however, are much more accepted in society than their male equivalents: "sissies."

The man who wrote the statements describing himself as someone who is sensitive and who cries easily is susceptible to being labeled a sissy. He is also susceptible to thinking of himself that way. And whereas there is relatively little shame in a girl being labeled a tomboy, especially in today's society, there is not yet equivalent acceptance for the boy who is labeled a sissy.

The reality of our lives is that while society is becoming more open and accepting of all kinds of differences, change happens slowly. And like it or not, gender stereotypes *do* persist.

Without fear of judgment, what do you think your reaction would be if you were a boy (or a man) whose personality included traits associated with being "sensitive," "thin-skinned," and "emotional." Would you be inclined to be proud of that? Or would you have mixed emotions about it? Might you even be a little embarrassed or ashamed about it? Most men I ask this question of respond that at best they would have mixed feelings about describing themselves that way, and some would actually be ashamed to be described that way. Yet those traits are characteristic of what it means to have MBPD. The man who wrote the statements cited previously was therefore actually very brave to do so.

Why Men Don't Seek Help

You've probably heard of cultures in which the concept of "face" is important, and in particular, the need to "save face." Saving face refers to the need to preserve and present a certain image to others (and also to one's self). For most men this means presenting a "face" that includes the following traits:

- Ruggedness: The opposite of being "sensitive" or "thin-skinned."

- Resilience: The ability to withstand stress without breaking down.

- Aggressiveness: The ability and willingness to use aggression to defend one's self as well as to be competitive in pursuing a goal.

- Independence: The idea of being self-sufficient, the so-called "captain of my ship."

Men vary with respect to just how much they feel a need to present themselves to others as well as to think of themselves in these terms. By the same token most men feel at least some need to present this type of "face" to the world and to see that "face" when they look in the mirror. Simply put, trying to live up to expectations and save face as a man is why men in general are much less willing to reach out for help—or admit that they need it—than are women. This accounts for such seemingly self-defeating "male behavior" as refusing to stop and ask for directions when they are driving and as a result ending up getting lost. Asking for directions would mean "losing face" for many men—so, they'd rather push on, finding their way through trial and error. This has infuriated millions of women. For these men (and lots of women) the invention of the Global Positioning System, or GPS, has been a gift from Heaven. The GPS allows men to find their destination without ever having to admit that they might be lost.

If men are reluctant to admit they are lost while driving, imagine how difficult it might be for them to admit that they might feel lost emotionally—out of control, emotionally "sensitive," or "thin-skinned." And now imagine how much harder it could be to admit that they have a flaw in their personality that is standing in the way of their ability to lead a fulfilling life.

Actually, it is not necessary to imagine how difficult it is, as research has demonstrated repeatedly that men are in fact more reluctant than women to seek help for emotional problems such as anxiety or depression. They also tend to strongly resist their partners' suggestions that they go for couple's counseling when their relationships are in crisis. As noted earlier, bouts of "free-floating anxiety" as well as depression are common among men who, as boys, experienced significant abuse, neglect, or rejection. And again, if men are reluctant to admit to and seek help for anxiety, depression, or relationship problems, imagine how resistant they could be to seeking help for a "personality disorder."

The unvarnished truth, then, is that men themselves actually contribute to the fact that MBPD is under-diagnosed, by virtue of their reluctance to admit to the exact symptoms that are associated with it, as well as their reluctance to seek help in general, for fear of losing face.

A Typical Case

Zack, now twenty-five, had never liked school much and had dropped out at the start of his senior high school year. Back then he'd had a small circle of friends with whom he mostly just hung out and smoked pot. In the summer months they would meet at a secluded clearing in the town park that was well known to other teens as a spot to get high. When the weather turned cold the small group would gravitate toward a detached garage that was adjacent to one of the boys' homes. According to Zack they did not interact. Rather, they literally just "hung out" together, the cannabis making them feel mellow. None of them did well in school, and only one member of this group actually graduated.

After dropping out, Zack spent the next year trying to find work that was both steady and paid more than minimum wage— without luck. In that way he discovered the harsh realities that face young uneducated men in our society. He was never hired full-time, and therefore never qualified for benefits such as medical insurance or even a single paid vacation or sick day. He never earned much more than minimum wage. And under those circumstances his dream of moving out of the house he shared with his mother, stepfather, and two younger half-brothers quickly faded.

That was also when Zack started drinking. His biological father had been an alcoholic and it seemed that Zack had inherited that man's capacity to tolerate large quantities of alcohol until he blacked out. Zack had had several such blackouts. Each time he was told by friends the next day what he and they had done the night before, but he'd have no memory of it.

Zack's relationship with his mother and stepfather gradually deteriorated over that year, to the point where on two occasions he moved in briefly with friends. Those welcomes inevitably wore out after a week or two, leaving Zack no choice but to return home. That was when he decided that he should drink and smoke less and return to school to earn his GED.

After getting his GED Zack took out a loan, enrolled in a training program, and became an HVAC (heating, ventilation, and air conditioning) technician with a specialty in servicing and repairing commercial heating and air conditioning systems. He continued to get high and drink, though not as often and not to the point of blacking out. He found, though, that if he did not drink or get high at all he was given to slipping into a state of melancholy. At that point he had his own apartment—a modest one-bedroom in a converted factory—and saw his family only rarely.

Zack met Sara just after he turned twenty-five. She was eighteen, had just graduated high school, and was set to attend a local community college with the goal of becoming a nurse. They met by chance when Zack came to work on the air conditioning system in her father's car dealership, where Sara worked during the summers. Zack took an immediate liking to Sara (and vice-versa) and by the time he finished his work at the car dealership they had spoken several times during his lunch break and he had her phone number.

Zack had dated a few girls in high school, as well as a couple since then, but none of these relationships had lasted long enough to become serious. Besides, Zack had been drinking alcohol, smoking pot, or both during much of that time. Now he wasn't using as much.

Sadly, the story of Zack and Sara did not have a happy ending. After six tumultuous months Sara decided to end it. She told Zack she was not yet ready for the kind of total commitment that she believed he was looking for. What Sara didn't say was that she had come to feel "smothered," and like a "prisoner" in that relationship, and that she was "burned out" trying to deal with Zack's moodiness, his hypersensitivity, and his possessiveness.

Sara decided to give this news to Zack over the phone. She'd already had some experience with his emotional volatility, which emerged only after they started dating and it became clear to Sara that Zack had serious feelings for her. Prior to dating he had impressed her as a polite, funny, attractive, and considerate young man whose rough times seemed to be behind him.

When Sara told Zack she wanted to break off their relationship he did not yell or threaten her; instead, his voice became solemn and he talked in ways that suggested he might do something to hurt himself. "He made statements like 'Life seems pointless now,' and he would not answer me when I asked him if he was going to be okay." To her later regret, Sara then told Zack he could come to her house so they could talk.

She let Zack in and led him to the family den. Initially Zack seemed outwardly depressed. He sat slumped on a couch in her family room, his eyes downcast, and when he spoke it was in a muted voice. Sara tried her best to be kind, telling Zack again that she was not ready for a commitment, and didn't think she would be for several years. That was when his mood, as Sara described it, "turned on a dime." He jumped up, started yelling at her, and accused her of leading him on. Then he accused her of cheating on him. "There's someone else, isn't there?" he said. "Tell me who it is!"

At that point Sara had heard enough. She also raised her voice and told Zack to leave. That was when he picked up a lamp and threw it. It flew past Sara's head and crashed against the wall. Then he overturned a coffee table. A few minutes later the police arrived on the scene. Sara's father, having heard Zack's escalating accusations, and fearing for his daughter's safety, had dialed 911.

Zack was arrested. His charges included assault (for throwing the lamp in Sara's direction), threatening, destruction of property, and trespassing. He spent that night in the local lockup. When he went to court the next day his case was continued. However, the judge issued a restraining order forbidding Zack from having any contact with Sara. He also ordered Zack to undergo a psychological evaluation and to follow any recommendations that came from that.

Zack's attorney told him that the ultimate disposition of his case would hinge on Zack's observing the restraining order and following through with counseling.

What happened next was typical for the vast majority of those with MBPD. Zack was interviewed. He was told that he had an "anger problem" and was probably also suffering from depression. He was told that he should attend an "anger management" program at a local clinic and also that he should consult with his primary care doctor about taking antidepressant medications.

Zack, following his attorney's advice, followed through on both recommendations. Did it help? No. Why? Because both the "diagnosis" and the "treatment" were off the mark. Neither stood to alter the borderline personality that was the cause of Zack's current problem (and which had also been the cause of what had essentially been a lost youth).

Misdiagnosed, Mistreated

MBPD is routinely misdiagnosed; therefore, whatever treatment men with this disorder get is aimed at surface issues as opposed to the root of the problem. Sure, Zack had acted aggressively toward Sara. But did he have an "anger management problem" in general? Not at all. He did not have a track record of getting into fights. He did not have trouble getting along with customers (though he privately thought some of them were jerks). He had never bullied anyone. It was only when faced with rejection that Zack had erupted that way.

According to Sara, Zack also became irritable and moody (though not violent) whenever he perceived that she was rejecting him, even when that had not been her intent. In her opinion Zack was hypersensitive to being ignored, to not getting the attention he wanted. Zack's supposed "anger problem," then, was situational and related to his core insecurity. Learning to "count to ten" (a common anger management technique) was not going to touch that hypersensitivity.

Zack could also get depressed, but his depression could evaporate as quickly as it overtook him. As Sara again attested, Zack could be "on top of the world" if he perceived that all was well between them and if he was happy with the work he was doing. But he could just as easily "fall off a cliff" into a deep funk if he felt that conditions between them were not good.

MBPD often creates a situation in which a man is his own worst enemy, because, as demonstrated above, men are reluctant to admit what is going on inside them, and what their core personality is truly like. We will look more at what goes on inside the MBPD man in the next chapter.

SUMMING UP

The traits and temperaments associated with MBPD in many ways run contrary to gender stereotypes about how men should be. This can, and often does, generate shame in MBPD men. In an effort to save face they may deny their sensitivity or their deep insecurity. Instead, they may be willing to accept a label of "antisocial personality," "depression," or "impulse control disorder." (And these sound much more macho or manly.) Such diagnoses can provide a convenient "cover" for the real issues. In Zack's case, for example, his charges were eventually resolved and he did no jail time. He stayed away from Sara, successfully completed his anger management program, and took antidepressant medication for a year. But his problems with relationships continued.

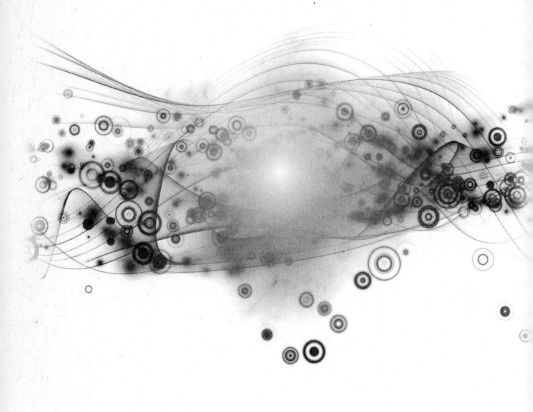

CHAPTER FOUR

The Spectrum of MBPD

The examples given so far all describe men who have what could be called moderate Male Borderline Personality Disorder. What does that mean? Simply put, Borderline Personality Disorder, whether in men or in women, does not refer to an "all or none" type of personality and temperament that a person either has or doesn't have. Rather, BPD is best thought of as existing on a spectrum.

MBPD: Not One-Size-Fits-All

For men with BPD, at one end of this spectrum is what I would call normal male insecurity. In other words, most if not all men can exhibit a few of the behaviors associated with BPD some of the time.

For example, we all may perceive that we are being rejected at times, when in fact we are not. We all may seek some attention from our loved ones at times. We all may feel jealous at times. And so on. However, at this end of the spectrum a man does not exhibit any of the behaviors that the men in our examples exhibit on a fairly regular and intense basis. From this baseline men's personalities can move more or less toward full-blown MBPD. In other words, there are different degrees of MBPD.

It is possible that you, as a man reading this book, may have a fairly severe form of MBPD, depending in large part on your past experiences. Or perhaps you believe that the man you love does. It is also possible that you have (or he has) a milder form of MBPD.

The examples given so far also illustrate some of the kinds of experiences that can lead to a man developing MBPD, namely rejection, abandonment, and abuse. As a reader of this book, whether you are male or female, chances are you have known at least one man who had at least a mild form of MBPD. And you may have been in a relationship with a man whose MBPD was fairly severe. Despite the fact that MBPD in men has received scant attention from professionals, it is rare that I speak with a person who has not had experience with at least one such man in a relationship.

The Faces of MBPD

Let's look at some of the ways in which Male Borderline Personality Disorder can show its face, along with ways it can vary in severity. Along the way we will look at a few more examples.

INSECURITY

Insecurity refers to a lingering feeling that you can't count on your loved one; that somehow you will be let down, rejected, or abandoned. For the person with MBPD, insecurity has its roots in actual experiences of this kind, though it may have no basis in that man's current relationship. Others may suffer the insecurity that comes from being treated with ambivalence: not knowing when they could count on comfort and support, and when they could not.

In some cases these experiences are truly severe. I've heard stories of men who were locked in a dark closet or basement as punishment. Others were beaten, while still others were deprived of food or shelter. Some were sexually molested. Many were ridiculed or bullied. On a less severe, but still damaging level, here is one man's story:

"My parents divorced when I was about six years old. For a while my father saw me pretty much every weekend. Then, after about a year, he moved out of state and I would see him every other weekend. That lasted maybe six months. But after he met the woman who eventually became his second wife, he would drive up to see me less and less. That was hard. The most difficult thing, though, was when he'd call and say he was coming up to see me. I would wait for him on the front porch, and he wouldn't show up. After a while my mother would come out and tell me to go inside, but I would insist on sitting there on the top step, sometimes for hours. I remember I didn't cry, but neither could I talk. I just felt so empty inside."

Did this man experience abandonment? He sure did. Was this abandonment as severe as being locked in a dark basement as punishment? Maybe not. But it's easy to see how it could sow the seeds of later insecurity—that feeling that your loved one can't be counted on.

In the case of Paul, mentioned earlier, he experienced abandonment fairly regularly. It happened whenever he was being beaten by his stepfather, and his mother would stand by instead of coming to his defense. It isn't difficult to imagine how these men's experiences, different as they are, could both lead to different degrees of the insecurity that is a central component of Borderline Personality Disorder.

Another way to think of insecurity is in terms of distrust. You can think of trust as a set of beliefs that

• Most people can be counted on to do what they say.

• Most people tend to be honest and trustworthy.

• Most people do not seek to take advantage of or abuse others.

Interestingly, research has shown that people who score higher on scales measuring trust tend to be better adjusted overall than those who do not. For example, they are less anxious, less prone to depression, and have more satisfying relationships. Distrustful people, in contrast, go through life in a guarded way, always vigilant against being taken advantage of, and hesitant to reach out for help. Does this describe you, or someone you love? If so, how distrustful do you think you may be: from extremely distrustful to mildly distrustful? How does your distrust affect your relationships? Does it bring you and your partner closer together or draw you further apart?

One final point is that most people are not consciously aware that they hold beliefs associated with distrust and insecurity. In other words, they do not walk around saying to themselves, "I can't count on my loved one to be there when I need her," or "My loved one will probably abandon me," or "My loved one will not tell me the truth." Rather, these beliefs tend to operate on an unconscious level and are reflected in our actions. Sometimes, for example, when they are asked to fill out a questionnaire or read a set of bullet points such as those just presented, a person will suddenly have an insight into just how distrustful or insecure they are. That insight can mark the starting point for change.

FREE-FLOATING ANXIETY

This second hallmark of Borderline Personality Disorder is directly linked to insecurity. Imagine that you are a man who goes through life believing that you can't count on loved ones to "watch your back" or be there when you need them. Imagine going through life with the unconscious belief that your loved one will lie to you or take advantage of you. What do you imagine your emotional state would be like?

Free-floating anxiety is a vague but persistent fear that hovers over a person or sits like a stone in his or her stomach. These individuals know they are uncomfortable, and they may even label that discomfort as anxiety, but they usually can't tell you what exactly they are anxious about. Sometimes they may grope for an explanation, but they are not sure what it is that is making them anxious.

Insecurity and distrust lead to free-floating anxiety, as well as to depression and anger. They can even lead to suicidal thoughts and actions. It all depends on how severe the insecurity and distrust are.

People deal with free-floating anxiety in different ways, and the prevailing ways of dealing with it tend to change over time. At one time eating disorders were exceptionally widespread among teens; today "cutting" is becoming predominant. Some of the ways men commonly try to conquer free-floating anxiety include

• Overeating (not as prevalent as in women but still there).

• Drinking.

• Smoking pot or taking tranquilizers or pain medication.

- Working excessive hours.

- Excessive exercise.

- Cutting.

The last of these—cutting—is most commonly associated with women who have BPD. I once asked a thirty-five year old woman with BPD how cutting her upper thighs (superficially) made her feel. She surprised me when she smiled broadly and said, "Wonderful! I love it!"

I asked the same question of an eighteen-year-old male I was counseling. Jared had been cutting his upper arms, using the tip of his old Boy Scout knife. He'd been doing this about twice a month for the past year. He thought the marks were hidden, but a female friend at school noticed them one day and told the school nurse, who in turn called Jared to her office and questioned him. That led to a call to Jared's parents, and shortly thereafter he landed in my office. Although Jared's response was somewhat less enthusiastic than the thirty-something woman's, he also said that cutting was a "stress reliever," by which he meant it provided temporary relief from his free-floating anxiety.

Free-floating anxiety is the manifestation of insecurity that seems to form the emotional backdrop for men with BPD. They may cope with it by drinking, by smoking pot, or by burying themselves in work. They may exercise compulsively or become compulsive about sex. At times when their anxiety peaks (usually in reaction to some unpleasant interaction with a loved one that sets off their insecurity) they may turn to cutting, seeking comfort through overeating, or burying their anxiety with alcohol or other drugs. If they perceive that they are being rejected or abandoned by a loved one (regardless of whether or not that is objectively true), they can also swing into either intense depression or intense anger. In the man with severe BPD that can include suicidal thoughts or actions, or violence.

SELF-HATRED

As discussed in the chapter on child development, abuse, rejection, and abandonment in our formative years typically leads to self-hatred. This self-hatred stems from the child's naïve assumption that if he is rejected, abandoned, or abused it must because he deserved it. So he grows up exaggerating whatever faults and flaws he does have, and hates himself for them. He will most likely also come up with a list of imagined shortcomings which, if he could only remedy them, he imagines would make him lovable. His thinking, (which he may be only dimly aware of) goes something like this, "If only I were smarter or stronger or taller or more athletic, etc., then I'd be okay and then I'd be lovable."

There are two types of self-hatred that I've heard expressed most often. The first is the "second-best" type of self-hatred. Marsha Linehan, a woman with BPD but also a psychologist who has pioneered treatment programs for women with BPD, gave a talk in 2011 at The Institute of Living in Hartford, Connecticut, where she disclosed she'd been a patient as a teen. Dr. Linehan described how, growing up, she'd long considered herself "second best" among her siblings. It was not clear exactly why she felt that way about herself. What about her family's dynamics had led to that self-image? Regardless of the reasons, the young Marsha was filled with self-hatred, and that self-hatred manifested itself in cutting, head-banging, and other self-abusive behaviors.

I have worked with men who similarly grew up feeling second best, and who also punished themselves for it. Brandon, for example, was a successful attorney who nonetheless was burdened with a second best self-image. The younger of two brothers, Brandon had grown up in the shadow of his athletically and socially gifted older brother, Carl. Here is how Brandon described it:

> "For as long as I could remember, the world, at least in my house, revolved around Carl. He was the apple of my parents' eyes, especially my father. When I was about ten my parents decided to finish the basement and make it into a recreation room. My father built a wet bar down there, complete with a mirrored wall and glass shelves. And on those shelves, beside the bottles of whiskey, were framed photos: of Carl playing football, Carl playing baseball, Carl receiving a Most Valuable Player Award. There were also trophies. I was not really into sports, so there weren't any trophies of mine. I think there was maybe one picture of me up there, but to be honest I wouldn't swear to it."

Brandon excelled in school, but for some reason that did not enthrall his father nearly as much as his brother Carl's athletic prowess. Also unlike Carl, Brandon never had a large circle of friends. The result was that Brandon grew up feeling more or less invisible.

Brandon's wife attested that she had seen (and dealt with) many of the symptoms associated with at least a mild form of MBPD in him. She described him this way:

> "Brandon is a very good attorney, but he is very hard on himself. He was merciless with himself when he was working toward becoming a partner in the firm. He kept comparing himself to others, and at one point I thought he might have a nervous breakdown when one of his peers made partner and he didn't. He made it the next year, but I'm not sure

Brandon is over that to this day. No matter how successful he is, for some reason it's never enough to satisfy him.

"Brandon is also a good man—a good husband and a good father. I know he loves me, and he loves our kids. He would do anything for us. Yet, he never seems at peace with himself. In our relationship he needs constant reassurance. I don't understand how a man can be so competent yet doubt himself so much. Also, he has something of a paranoid side—he likes to check my cell phone and email accounts, and he often asks me where I've been if I'm ten minutes late coming home."

Brandon suffered from the "second best" form of self-hatred. It's a form of self-torture that is manifested first and foremost in a man who is not able to be at peace with himself. No matter what he does, it just isn't enough. Many men's physical health suffers as a result of the chronic stress this type of self-hatred creates.

A second type of self-hatred I've seen many times is the "damaged goods" variety. When therapists are dealing with a woman who has a diagnosis of BPD one of the possibilities they think of is the possibility that she was sexually molested or assaulted. The self-hatred that many such women experience, as a result of abuse, is referred to as the "damaged goods syndrome." This was no doubt even more strongly the case when women were expected to remain sexually innocent prior to marriage, but it remains true today that many women who have been victimized blame themselves and/or feel they have somehow been "soiled."

Men can also suffer from the damaged goods syndrome. Without diminishing or making light of the effects of sexual, emotional, and physical abuse of girls, it should be noted that boys also suffer these experiences and their effects, and in far larger numbers than are reported. In part because of the gender misperceptions discussed in Chapter Three, boys rarely report it when they are sexually assaulted, physically abused, or bullied. So these events are more common than many people want to believe. Consider, for example, the recent arrest and eventual conviction of a well-known college football coach for abusing numerous young boys over a period of fifteen years. Consider also the recent scandals involving pedophile priests. Many of their victims were boys. These scandals are a testament to how the abuse of boys remains a largely hidden problem in our society.

The reason it is hidden relates back to the sex-role stereotypes discussed earlier, in particular the stereotype that boys, because they like rough-and-tumble play and are prone to taking risks, are also emotionally tough and resilient. Believing that about themselves, boys are apt to feel shame when they are the victims of bullying or abuse—because a man (or a boy) ought to be able to defend himself. That shame keeps them from speaking out.

There may be as many men with MBPD who have experienced sexual abuse as there are women and, therefore, as many men as women who secretly regard themselves as damaged goods. For a man like this, disclosing his past abuse to a trusted individual can mark the beginning of the journey out of Borderline Personality Disorder. But this is exceedingly difficult for a man to do. It means finding the courage to let go of sex-role stereotypes and expectations that are not based in reality but have a long tradition behind them. In recent years more men have found that courage. Some have joined together to seek justice. And some I have worked with have begun that journey of healing, which begins by recognizing the insidious damaged-goods syndrome, re-examining their beliefs about what it means to be a man, and revising their self-image.

JEALOUSY

The insecurity that lurks at the core of the MBPD personality also drives these men to be jealous and possessive. Who would not be jealous or envious if, deep down, they believed that they were either "second best" or "damaged goods"? Living life that way, it's easy to see how someone could expect that anything of value could be taken away. And, it would not be difficult for him to believe that a loved one could be lured away by someone who is better than he is, or who had more to offer than he did.

Jealousy has been called "a green-eyed monster." Whatever the color of its eyes, at mild levels, a little jealousy can be considered flattering. It can be interpreted as meaning that we are desirable. Who among us has not used jealousy at one time or another to "test" just how interested someone else was in us? I've interviewed many women who ended up in relationships with MBPD men, but who at first found their jealousy gratifying. As one woman, Judy, put it, "I had come off a couple of relationships where I felt that I had put in more than I got back. I had been the pursuer, and I got taken advantage of. So when I met Mark and I could tell that he was jealous of this male friend I'd had a platonic relationship with for years, part of me liked that. It said to me that Mark was attracted to me and wanted me."

If Mark's jealousy had remained within reasonable bounds it might not have become a problem in his relationship with Judy. Unfortunately, his jealousy crossed the line, from flattering to smothering. This pathological level of jealousy leads the person with MBPD to become overly possessive and intrusive. Here are a few typical examples of pathological jealousy:

• Insisting on having access to a loved one's phone messages and records.

- Wanting to sift through a loved one's emails and read them at will.

- Asking for access to all credit card, banking, and other financial records.

- Making frequent phone calls to a loved one when he or she is out with friends.

- Questioning where a loved one has been, or grilling the person when he or she is even a few minutes late.

- Criticizing the clothing a loved one chooses to wear, and/or insisting on being the one who chooses that clothing.

- Criticizing a loved one's choice in friends, and/or attempting to break up such friendships.

- Viewing a loved one's family or friends as threats to the relationship.

Of course, there may be instances in which friends (or family members) do indeed disapprove of a relationship we may have. Their own jealousy and insecurity may be the reason. It may also be the case that a friend or family member's dislike is based on a perception that a relationship with a man with Borderline Personality Disorder is indeed a problematic one. In other words, it is based on a gut feeling that this relationship is not a good one. One mother described her perception this way:

"It didn't take me long to sense that Carmen's relationship with Javier was going to be a problem. I'd made it my habit, though, never to question Carmen on her choices in boyfriends, for the obvious reason—I was afraid it would make her like them more!

"Javier came on strong, which at the time I could see appealed to Carmen. She's a beautiful, bright young

woman, but for some reason she didn't have much luck with the boys she dated through high school and college. I think she was a bit naïve and ended up dating some 'bad boys,' if you know what I mean—even if they were college students.

"When Carmen first started dating Javier I was open to the idea that maybe she had found a good relationship, finally. I knew that Carmen was sometimes more into a relationship than her boyfriend was. A few weeks into her relationship with Javier, Carmen told me that they were spending almost all their free time together. I was aware that she wasn't spending much time at home, other than to get home from work, shower, and change clothes.

"Two of Carmen's previous boyfriends had either cheated on her or at least flirted with other women. She found it appealing, I think, that Javier seemed to have eyes only for her and wanted to be with her so much. As it turned out, though, Javier quickly became smothering.

"After a while Carmen would tell me about how Javier would call her cell phone every half hour if she wanted to do some shopping by herself, or even if she met a girlfriend for coffee. Then Carmen let on once that Javier had questioned her about whether she and I were too close. That troubled me.

"About a year later Carmen finally broke it off with Javier. She eventually confided that she'd tried to do that a couple of times before, but that each time he'd pleaded with her and she would relent and take him back. I suspect that there may also have been one occasion when Javier *may have even threatened suicide in order to get Carmen to change her mind."*

The kind of jealousy and possessiveness that Javier expressed should not be mistaken for love. Those who find themselves on the receiving end of such behavior do not feel loved. What they do feel is smothered. They compare it to being in a prison. Pathological jealousy is a total invasion of privacy. It fails to recognize that there are any "boundaries" separating us as individuals.

Confusing Sex with Intimacy

Men and women tend to think of intimacy in somewhat different ways. We will devote a whole chapter to this in Part Two. For now, suffice it to say that men (and to some extent women) with Borderline Personality Disorder often confuse sex with intimacy. In other words, they try to compensate for loneliness, anxiety, and/or insecurity through sex.

Surely sexual intimacy can be an incredibly important part of a relationship. It is one way that we and our loved one can get close and, in a sense, become "one." At the same time, people have always turned to sex, at least at some times, to relieve stress, as well as for comfort. But for the man who struggles with Borderline Personality Disorder, sex can become a way in which he feels reassured that he is still loved. It can become a means of reducing, at least for a while, free-floating anxiety.

And what happens if a man with MBPD needs such reassurance that he is loved, or seeks sex as an antidote for anxiety, daily? Or, twice a day? Partners I have interviewed and who have loved a man with MBPD have expressed reactions ranging from sadness to pity to outright anger at having to provide such reassurance through sex. Again, here is a typical story:

As often happens, Shana met Martin, on the rebound. She'd married, then divorced James, a man who, among other issues, had little interest in sex. "The funny thing is," Shana told me, "that I knew from the beginning that James wasn't very interested in sex. In the beginning we did have sex, and fairly often, but it was sort of perfunctory. I remember thinking that maybe it would get better over time, that James was probably just not that experienced—or that he was shy. I was just kidding myself. Now I go by the rule, 'What you see is what you will get.'

"Of course sex didn't change. In fact it got worse. Then, after Alex was born, it stopped altogether. We went to see a therapist, but still nothing changed. James promised to do the 'sensual massages' that the therapist prescribed, but I think we only did it once or twice. I'd have to be the one to bring it up, and James would either have an excuse—usually, work to do—or else he would do it without enthusiasm. At one point I told my therapist that I had decided I could just do without sex—that it was not particularly enjoyable, and that it wasn't all that important to me. I remember the therapist looking at me skeptically."

After their divorce, when Shana started dating Martin, she was pleasantly surprised at how interested he was in making love to her—again, and again, and again. After they'd been together about six months, however, Shana began to realize that Martin's desire for sex was not just driven by attraction. "Sure, he's attracted to me," she explained, "but I also can see clearly now how Martin turns to sex whenever he is feeling tense, also just as a way of knowing that I still love him."

Just how much of a problem is using sex for reassurance? Well, most people have done that at times. The issue is *how often* we turn to sex for reassurance and comfort, or as a cure for anxiety, and *how long* that reassurance and comfort lasts. According to Shana, for Martin it did not last and the result was that he'd approach her for sex every day. If she responded that she was tired (or just not in the mood) he would get irritable.

When we last spoke, Shana told me she was not sure if she wanted to remain in the relationship with Martin. She was already starting to feel her own sexual desire waning. "It's like his interest isn't flattering any more. I see it as a kind of desperate need on his part. Also, I don't have time to experience my own sexual desire," she said, "because I'm always satisfying Martin's sexual needs."

For men, perhaps more so than for women, intimacy includes a physical element. Whereas women are generally able to feel close not only through affection and sex, but also through talking and doing activities together, men seem to rely more on physical closeness to experience the warmth, comfort, and closeness that defines intimacy. In the MBPD man this need can grow out of proportion and, ironically, end up creating distance where closeness is what is sought. In some cases it can also lead to reckless and risky behavior, for example turning to prostitutes to satisfy unmet intimacy needs or relief from anxiety and insecurity, or having thoughtless, unprotected sex for the same reason.

BLACK-AND-WHITE THINKING

Here again, insecurity shows itself as the culprit. The man whose personality and temperament fit the borderline profile is a man who is on the lookout for rejection, abuse, and/or abandonment. As anyone who has been in a relationship with such a man will tell you, he sometimes will perceive such a rejection or abandonment when none was intended. For example, one woman told me that being distracted by tending to a child or being engaged in a phone conversation with a friend, when her MBPD husband returned home from work, was enough to trigger a reaction nearly as strong as if she had gone out to dinner and not informed him. "He needs my attention as soon as he walks through the door. If he doesn't get it he'll immediately fall into a sulk. Later on he'll snap at me. It took me a long time to figure out what was going on. Now, as much as possible, I just give him a minute or two of attention and he seems fine."

The above example illustrates the kind of black-and-white thinking that is common in men with MBPD. From their point of view you are either their friend or their enemy. Their radar is forever scanning for rejection or for being let down, and their emotions are consequently set on a hair trigger to respond.

To gain more insight into whether MBPD describes you, ask yourself the following questions:

- How "thin-skinned" are you? Are you easily slighted?

- Are you slow to forgive when you feel slighted? Do you hold a grudge?

- Do you have many, few, or no long-term friendships?

Naturally, we are all capable of being thin-skinned at times. We attribute intentions to others' words and actions all the time, and we all can sometimes misperceive someone else's words or actions. However, to the extent to which the above describes you, or someone you love, you or he may possess this quality that defines MBPD.

Remember that MBPD is not an all-or-nothing personality type. The man who occasionally misinterprets a loved one's actions and who feels hurt as a result does not necessarily have a full-fledged borderline personality. There are many shades of gray between "normal human insecurity" and full-blown MBPD.

It's important, therefore, to keep the above in perspective as you think about whether you or someone you love has MBPD, and if so how severe it is.

POOR EMOTIONAL CONTROL

Free-floating anxiety, bouts of depression, possibly including suicidal thoughts, anger that seems unprovoked, or mood swings, these are also part and parcel of MBPD. And as is true for jealousy and all the other personal qualities associated with MBPD, this poor emotional control exists on a spectrum. The most severe cases of MBPD can have so little emotional control that sustaining a relationship becomes virtually impossible. In moderate forms, those who love a man with MBPD report that they must spend unpredictable amounts of time "walking on egg shells" in order to avoid setting off an unpleasant episode. Some people do this for a long time, while others decide, sooner or later, to throw in the towel.

Then there are those whose MBPD is relatively mild, and who are most likely to be described using terms such as "touchy" or "moody." Todd was one of those men whose personality and temperament fell somewhere in the middle ground between normal human insecurity and full-blown MBPD.

Todd was a physical therapist whose specialty was post-surgery rehabilitation. Twice divorced and the father of one child from each marriage, Todd had lived alone for two years. In that time he had occupied himself primarily between long hours at work—even signing up for additional specialized training—and spending time with his children.

Todd met Pamela at one of the professional workshops he was attending. She was also a physical therapist, and because she was drawn to the area of sports injuries, she also worked with many postoperative patients. She and Todd had clicked immediately, spending time together over lunches and breaks at the conference, and by the time they departed they had each others' numbers as well as a commitment to get together soon.

That was when Todd decided to see a therapist. Looking back he could see how he'd contributed to his divorces. "When I am in a situation like work," he explained, "I tend to be cool as a cucumber. Patients like me because I calm them down, and the work I do with them helps them recover their range of motion, and sometimes even their ability to walk. But when I get into a relationship I change. Both of my exes have described me as a Jekyll-and-Hyde."

Todd's personal background was not unlike that of many men with MBPD, though perhaps a bit less severe. He had been the youngest of two children. His father had been a successful businessman, but also one whose work demanded frequent travel. Todd described his mother this way: "Mom was basically a sweet sort of person. But she liked to drink, especially when my father was away, which was often. I can remember many times, getting off the school bus and letting myself into the house, and finding my mother asleep—actually, passed out—on the family room couch. This did not happen every day, but it happened at least a couple of times a week."

Todd said that on those days when his mother was unconscious he and his older sister pretty much fended for themselves. His sister usually made dinner (for themselves as well as their mother), then they would do their respective homework before watching television.

"I think my sister must have been very angry at my mother," Todd explained, "because she could be very nasty to me. She did that mostly when my mother wasn't there to see it. My sister had lots of friends, but she hardly ever had a friend over. I think that was probably because she was embarrassed about my mother and could never be sure if she'd be sober or passed out when we got home."

Todd's sister's "nastiness" included bossing him around and making fun of him. And because neither of his parents was able to protect him (his father being away much of the time, and his mother often passed out) Todd had little choice but to endure a situation that was at least moderately abusive. That was most likely what lay at the root of his tendency to exhibit many of the signs of MBPD, including his "moodiness."

Not long after Todd felt attracted to a woman, and seriously interested in a relationship with her, his "moodiness" would gradually emerge. He admitted that the phrase "thin-skinned" accurately described him. "It feels like I can't really control it," he said. "I know it must be my insecurity. But I just find myself feeling jealous. With Pam I know I'd get jealous of any men she worked with, and any man she called a friend."

Aside from his jealousy Todd found that he'd looked to his ex-wives for approval. "I mean constant approval," he added. "To the point where I believe they started to lose respect for me — because I didn't seem to have much self-esteem."

When I asked Todd if he had similar experiences in his relationships with his children he replied, after reflecting for a moment, "Well, I certainly like their approval. But I don't relate to feeling insecure in my relationships with them. They love me, and I love them, period."

That insight proved to be the point of departure for Todd to begin the work of overcoming his Borderline Personality Disorder. It is a question that we all should ask ourselves every so often: Who in my life has ever loved me, period?

SUBSTANCE ABUSE AND BEHAVIORAL ADDICTION

Addiction is said to be "one disease with many manifestations," and in our society we see evidence of that all around us. Perhaps it's due to our abundance and affluence relative to the rest of the world; but whatever the reason, when we have emotional discomfort, we certainly have an excess of substances we can use to "fix" or self-medicate.

- We can get addicted to food and become obese. We may then turn to a series of diets in an effort to control our food addiction, in much the same way as an alcoholic tries to "control" his or her drinking.

- We consume more antianxiety medications than the rest of the world combined, and we can easily become addicted to these medications.

- We can become addicted to exercise, past the point where we are maintaining optimal health, but instead actually doing harm to ourselves.

- We can become addicted to cutting or otherwise abusing our bodies.

- Hoarding, gambling, plastic surgery—the list of manifestations of addiction can be extended *ad infinitum.*

Men and women who have BPD often turn to substances or behaviors that are addictive in an attempt to relieve or escape free-floating anxiety. You'll recall that this refers to the vague but nagging fear a person can experience without being able to name the source or cause of that fear. One young man, Seth, who had some borderline traits, spoke with me about cutting his arms with sharp objects such as a razor blade, or sometimes a paper clip. He did not cut himself deeply, typically not going deep enough to bleed, but enough to create a visible scratch. When his parents took notice that their son had many such scratches on both his arms they confronted him and insisted he see a therapist.

I asked Seth to describe a typical episode of "cutting" for me. I learned that it involved something akin to a ritual, but always in the background there was free-floating anxiety. I was not sure where that came from, though Seth did admit that he was more or less an "outcast" at school, and that at lunchtime he was relegated to a table shared by other "outcasts."

In any case, the ritual Seth followed began with the free-floating anxiety building inside him. Seth would then contain it, by sheer willpower, for as long as he could. At some point, though, he'd make a conscious decision to "drain away" (his words) his anxiety. That's when he would go into his room, close the door, sit at his desk, and cut himself. After doing so he would feel better, sometimes for a week or more. But the anxiety would always eventually catch up to him.

SUMMING UP

In this chapter we've taken what could be called an "inside look" at the man who struggles with Borderline Personality Disorder. And struggle he does. Men with BPD may not use that term to diagnose themselves—but make no mistake, they are unhappy on some deep level, and they know it. Some men describe it as an "emptiness that won't go away."

Borderline personality disorder exists on a spectrum that can vary from relatively mild to very severe. Not all those with MBPD exhibit every one of the behaviors and traits associated with it. Similarly, not every man with BPD will exhibit these traits with the same intensity. The point is that while MBPD is clearly identifiable, it is a mistake to consider men with MBPD as being identical to one another. In this case, as in most other cases, stereotyping is not helpful.

CHAPTER FIVE

Taking Stock: Where Are You on the MBPD Spectrum?

We will shortly get to the issue of coping with and even overcoming Borderline Personality Disorder. Part Two will present a series of solutions. These solutions can be used by men who identify themselves as having some of the traits and temperaments associated with MBPD. Those solutions, however, can also be very helpful to those who find themselves in a relationship with the MBPD man. In effect, they provide many guidelines for what to do (and what *not* to do) to help a man avoid getting pulled down into the mire that is MBPD.

Before we do that, however, it can be a useful first step to take a few minutes to take stock—of yourself or of someone you love—to determine if MBPD describes you or him, and if so to what extent. In other words, change begins with some insight or awareness. If I don't realize I have a bad temper, for example, or that I have a deep distrust of others, I won't have much motivation to change that, or any idea of how to do so. In a way, having MBPD is not unlike being an addict, in that both MBPD and addiction wreak havoc in a person's life. However, just as the addict will not get into recovery and experience a better life until he "connects the dots" and realizes that addiction is responsible for the havoc in his life, an awareness of the connection between the various aspects of MBPD and their consequences marks a vital starting point for change.

The MBPD Inventory

What follows is a questionnaire: *The MBPD Inventory*. It consists of a summary of all the behaviors and temperaments associated with MBPD that have been discussed so far. Keep in mind that MBPD is not an all-or-none, one-size-fits-all personality type; rather, it describes a personality/temperament that can vary in form as well as in intensity. Not every man with the disorder will exhibit all of the signs of MBPD, nor will every man exhibit them with the same intensity. Accordingly, you will be asked to estimate not only which issues are relevant for you (or your loved one) but also to what extent they are present, from "not at all" to "extremely."

When you have finished, you will have a total score. Equally important, you will have in your hands a profile that can then guide you as you work through the various solutions provided in Part Two. I suggest using a journal if you have one or you can jot down the numbers of your answers on a separate piece of paper, where you can also do the addition.

The MBPD Inventory

For each item, indicate to what extent it describes you (or someone you love). Use the scale below to rate yourself (or loved one) for each statement.

0	1	2	3	4	5	6	7	8	9	10

NOT AT ALL   SOMEWHAT   EXTREMELY

FREE-FLOATING ANXIETY

You feel anxious at times but you can't name what you are anxious about or what you fear. Some people experience this kind of anxiety as a form of "dread," like something bad is about to happen.

THIN-SKINNED

Your feelings tend to be easily hurt. You are very sensitive to criticism or rejection.

INSECURE AND DISTRUSTFUL

You are not sure that your loved ones or friends can be counted on when the chips are down. In other words, you are not confident that they "have your back." On some level you believe they are capable of abandoning you.

JEALOUS

You harbor fears that your loved one might cheat on you or leave you. You envy other men for how successful or popular they are compared to you.

SELF-HATRED

Words like "second best" or "damaged goods" describe how you think of yourself. You are self-critical.

SELF-DESTRUCTIVE

You have abused alcohol or other drugs, have intentionally hurt yourself (cutting), or otherwise been harmful to your health (binge eating, etc.)

BLACK-AND-WHITE THINKING

You have a tendency to categorize people as either friends or enemies. You have a hard time tolerating differences of opinion between yourself and a loved one. You are not only quick to feel that a friend or loved one has let you down, but you hold onto a grudge. It's as if you believe on some level that if someone close to you has let you down or disappointed you in some way you can never trust them again.

APPROVAL/ATTENTION SEEKING

You crave approval, attention, and love. You can be overly accommodating in order to get these items or feelings. Alternatively, you may do something negative, such as threatening to hurt yourself, in order to get attention.

CONFUSING SEX WITH INTIMACY

You look at sex as the primary means through which a loved one expresses love for you. If you are feeling anxious you seek sex to make that anxiety go away.

MOODY

You respond to emotional triggers abruptly. For example, you may become enraged in response to a minor disappointment; or the same disappointment could send you into a state of depression.

Your MBPD Score and Profile: What Do They Mean?

Speaking strictly quantitatively, your score (or your loved one's score) on the MBPD Inventory can vary anywhere from 0 to 100. Obviously, the lower the overall MBPD score is, the less that personality and temperament type fits the individual. In contrast, the higher the score the more that person fits the MBPD profile. Very high scores—say over seventy-five—may indicate that the help of a skilled therapist is needed in order to successfully break free from MBPD. These men tend to be very unhappy and self-destructive, as well as incapable of sustaining fulfilling relationships. Their MBPD stands between them and any reasonable definition of happiness.

What about those in the middle? What about the man with an MBPD score of thirty? Or fifty? Well, these men are suffering as well. However, as opposed to a man with an MBPD score of eighty or more (who may indeed be "impossible to love"), these mid-range men are what I mean by "hard to love."

The MBPD profile you have just produced also serves to illustrate how MBPD is not an all-or-none phenomenon. Very likely your (or your loved one's) MBPD profile will be unique to you or him, and different from other men's profiles. This is very important because it can help you identify which issues are the most important (and most problematic) and which should receive priority. That is true whether you choose to work on the solutions in Part Two by yourself (or together with your loved one), or whether you choose to find a therapist to help you.

Your MBPD profile is important. Keep it in mind as you move into Part Two. At this point, assuming you have done an honest MBPD Inventory, you now have a sense of what issues you need to work on in order to improve your life, your relationships, and your chances for achieving happiness and serenity.

PART TWO

SOLUTIONS FOR MBPD MEN

(AND THOSE WHO LOVE THEM)

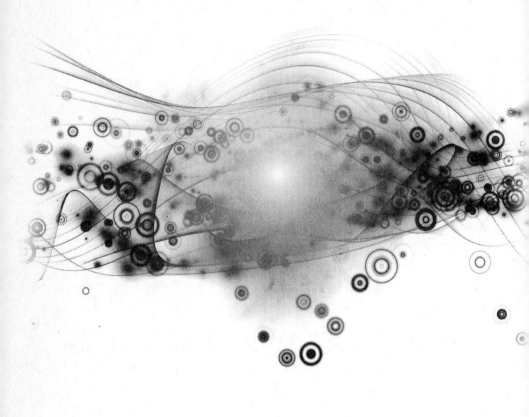

CHAPTER SIX

Managing Free-Floating Anxiety

Brent, now forty-four and a tenured professor in a community college, described the family he grew up in this way:

"My mother was chronically depressed; I mean seriously depressed. Most days when I came home from school she would be in bed sleeping. And when she did get out of bed she mostly just sat around in a housedress. My grandmother, my mom's mother, lived with us and mostly took care of me and my brother. She wasn't exactly warm and cuddly, though, if you know what I mean. And she liked her brandy.

"I was the oldest, my brother was kind of limited, and I was the one who was expected to look after him. He tagged along frequently, which kind of cramped my social life, but I didn't mind it that much.

"My father worked two jobs, and though he didn't drink he wasn't much interested in being a father either. He'd come home, eat a quick dinner, and head off to his second job. We saw him on weekends, but we didn't interact much even then. He took me and my brother to a couple of minor league baseball games, which stands out as the highlight of my childhood.

"I did well in school but I was a skinny, frail kid, so I got picked on a lot. What I remember most about school is feeling anxiety every day that I was going to get picked on. That went on for a long time. The couple of times I told my father about it he frowned and told me to give the bully a bloody nose. The bullies were always a lot bigger than me, so that never happened.

"My brother and I were never beaten at home, and there was always food on the table, but our house was emotionally cold and empty. I'd be surprised if more than a dozen words were exchanged on some days.

"I was around ten when I started my rituals. I remember praying to God and telling him that if he kept the bullies away from me that day I would say so many prayers. Eventually I started trading rituals—like kneeling on the sidewalk in back of our house every morning—in exchange for God keeping the bullies away. I would kneel there and it would hurt, but that was what I thought God wanted so that he would keep the bullies away.

"Looking back on it I think the bullying stopped because I did grow some and the bullies probably found someone else *to pick on. Either that or they got bored with me. But at the time I thought it was my 'sacrifices' that were protecting me.*

"I recall feeling anxious pretty much all the time as a kid. I couldn't seem to relax at all. Again, there was one time when I couldn't stand it anymore. I must have been around thirteen. I opened up and told my father that I was incredibly unhappy. I told him I thought I needed help. That time he didn't just frown, he got noticeably angry. 'No son of mine is going to see a psychiatrist!' he said. 'Just get with the program. You've got nothing to be unhappy about!'"

After he entered college, Brent began to experience periodic bouts of depression that would sap his energy and sometimes make it difficult for him to get out of bed and go to classes. Consequently his grades slipped a bit, though he did manage to maintain a B+/A- average. He went to see a counselor at the college, who sent him to a psychiatrist, who prescribed an antidepressant along with antianxiety medication. The psychiatrist was kind, but he spent only half an hour with Brent. He explained that because depression ran in Brent's family (his mother), Brent might need to stay on those medications indefinitely. Brent met with a counselor a few times after that, but mostly he discussed his medications: if he was taking them, if he was experiencing any negative side effects, and if his anxiety and depression seemed to be lessening.

Did Brent suffer from depression? Yes. Did he also suffer from free-floating anxiety? Again the answer is yes. That being said, was medication likely to be enough to rid Brent of his demons? Probably not. Yet when Brent and I met he still carried the official diagnoses of "depressive disorder" and "anxiety disorder." No one had ever mentioned Borderline Personality Disorder to him; consequently, he had never pursued counseling with any consistency.

Should Brent have stopped taking medication? Probably not, at least not until he was well into counseling focused on helping him to deal with his MBPD. Over time, though, some men are able to either decrease or stop their dependence on medications as they get a better handle on their MBPD.

What motivated Brent to seek counseling now was a renewed bout of severe free-floating anxiety that seemed clearly linked to two things. The first was that he had recently been asked to head up a committee that would be responsible for the college's four-year reaccreditation review. Indeed, this was a major responsibility (but also a feather in his cap).

The second issue was what Brent described as a deteriorating marriage and home life. "My wife says that I never seem present anymore when I'm home. This is nothing totally new. It's been somewhat of a longstanding issue for me. I know I can be distracted, and usually it has to do with the fact that I can never seem to leave work at work. It's gotten worse over the past four months since I took on this committee. I'd prefer to quit it, but that would be a major embarrassment. Now I'm committed to it for the next year."

Brent and his wife Karen had two daughters. He said he loved Karen and that having children was the best thing that had ever happened to him. Still, he knew that even the girls were aware that their father was often distracted—"out to lunch" was the phrase they used. Apparently Brent was now "out to lunch" so much of the time that Karen was getting increasingly angry. She accused him of not listening to her, of not being interested in the family, and of being "married" to his job. While he did not believe that this meant that Karen was interested in a divorce, her unhappiness was very evident, according to Brent. And it worried him. As distracted as he might be, he was nevertheless aware of her being distant when they were together.

Up until the time he met Karen, Brent explained, he had not dated much. "I was not totally inexperienced," he said, "but the few relationships I had didn't last long. After a while I realized that it probably was my insecurity that ruined them. I was always very jealous, always looking for reassurance; I tended to be the smothering type. I think that turned women off. I tried to tone that down with Karen, and I believe to some extent I did. But I remember worrying at times that she would leave me. And I've always avoided any kind of confrontation. Instead, if I am unhappy about something, I'll brood and get depressed instead of trying to do something about it. Karen is a good woman, and she loves me. But over time she took charge in the marriage, and also over the girls."

In a session together, Karen affirmed Brent's insecurity. "He's always been a bit clingy," she said, "but that got better, especially after the girls came along. I think fatherhood has been good for Brent. And the girls adore him, even though he often seems distracted. I know they wish he would work less when he's at home, but Brent has always been super-conscientious. It's rare that he doesn't spend at least a couple of hours a night on his laptop. I think that's how he deals with his insecurities at the college, too. It's become worse, though, since he took on this new responsibility at the college. He always gets high ratings from his students, and praise from his dean, but I know he still has doubts about his ability. He can be awfully self-critical."

Dealing with Free-Floating Anxiety

So Brent, intelligent and successful as he was, was nevertheless burdened by a Borderline Personality Disorder that was probably of moderate intensity. His dominant personality trait was his insecurity, which lies at the core of every man (and woman) with

BPD. Judging by his autobiography it isn't a stretch to see how the youthful Brent could grow to become a man with MBPD.

Now that Brent finally knew what he was dealing with—MBPD—as well as some idea of why he would be the way he was, the question then became one of what to tackle first, and how. Although there were certainly several issues that Brent could work on, I've often found it helpful when counseling MBPD men to begin with any free-floating anxiety that may be haunting them. It is difficult, in fact, to make much headway in other areas, such as working on trust or jealousy, while free-floating anxiety is unchecked. For that reason I thought it best to start this second half of the book by looking at free-floating anxiety: where it comes from, and what a man can do to control it.

ORIGINS OF FREE-FLOATING ANXIETY

The example of Brent illustrates how a boy can develop free-floating anxiety that he then carries into adulthood. None of the significant adults in young Brent's life—his mother, his maternal grandmother, or his father—were what you could call consistent sources of nurturance, support, or protection for him. Sure, Brent and his brother were fed regular meals, and they each had a bed to sleep in. But creating a secure and confident child requires more than food and shelter. It requires, first, relationships with one or more adult caretakers with whom the child can communicate openly (and feel heard). It is in this relational context that a child discovers his "voice." If he can tell a caring adult when he is frightened, for example, or when he feels lonely, and then feels that the adult understands and will be his advocate (and protector if necessary), that builds security.

But what happened when Brent attempted to express his feelings to his father, to tell this man who could have been his advocate and protector, first, that he was afraid of the bullies and, later, that he was deeply unhappy? His father's reaction essentially told Brent not to talk about it, and to handle it by himself. Since sharing our feelings can in itself be helpful (consider what the essence of psychotherapy is), Brent was locked out from this way of building a sense of security. So he learned to keep his feelings to himself. Indeed, he told me, he learned not to think much about how or what he was feeling.

Second, a child builds self-confidence when he has a secure relational base from which to venture forth into the social world. That social world, as Brent discovered early on, is not all peachy-rosy; on the contrary, it is as fraught with dangers and threats as it is with opportunities and adventures. There have always been bullies, to be sure, but the secure child knows he can turn to one or more adults for protection and comfort.

Imagine this scenario: a child of about seven years of age experiences a bout of nightmares. He awakens and pads into his parents' bedroom and wakes up his father and mother. One of them listens to his tale. Then they either let him sleep in the bed between them, or one of them goes and lies in his bed with him until he is sound asleep. In later years, as he grows older, he's fine with having his mom or dad tuck him back into his own bed, while leaving a night light on.

Imagine how the child might have felt and responded if he had been chastised for being afraid, or simply told to go back to bed. Despite the concerns of some parents, children who are comforted when they are afraid almost never develop a habit of consistently waking them up or wanting to sleep in their bed. Like all healthy children, this child wanted to sleep in his own bed, in his own room, and he gravitated naturally to that. Because his parents were a safe "base" that he could turn to when needed—a place where he could get comfort and feel safe—he did not need that comfort often, and he needed it less as he grew to become an independent, adventurous, and social child.

Not so for Brent, who nodded in agreement when I suggested that childhood, for him, was like being cast into the wilderness and left to fend for himself. No one was interested in hearing about his anxieties, and there was no one to turn to for protection or solace. No wonder he lived under the specter of anxiety. Indeed, as a child he was vulnerable, and he could become a victim at any time.

Brent's anxiety carried on into his relationships, where he sought the comfort and security that he longed for. He did this on an unconscious level, however. He had never actually articulated how he felt, or made the connection between his adult anxiety and insecurity, his lack of secure attachments as a child, and the comfort he sought in his relationships. As he had done as a child, Brent sought to insulate and protect himself, not through religious rituals but through working compulsively.

If you suffer, as Brent did, from free-floating anxiety—whether often or only occasionally—it can be helpful to take a moment to reflect on its origins. This anxiety, which people generally consider as having no identifiable source, usually does in fact have such a source. It's just been forgotten. Research has shown that all of us actually have a fairly incomplete memory of our formative years. Isolated events may stand out, but as a historical record memories tend to be rather unreliable and incomplete. For men and women with BPD this is even more the case. This was true for Brent, who had not thought much about what life had been like for him as a boy.

The source of free-floating anxiety is usually no mystery; it has its roots in insecurity of the kind that had dogged Brent all those years. As a healthy adult man (and one who did not resemble the frail boy he'd once been), Brent was no longer afraid of being bullied. On the contrary, he was both physically and intellectually fit, able to fend for himself in any likely situation. His anxiety, rather, was a leftover from his years of living an insecure life in a family that was mostly devoid of real love, affection, and support.

This insight alone was enough to give Brent a small "handle" on his anxiety. He could then use that handle to challenge his anxiety whenever it occurred. You can do this as well. If you believe your free-floating anxiety is linked to insecurity, see if you are able to make any connections, to determine where in your experiences that insecurity had its beginnings. Now, moving forward, when you feel that free-floating anxiety starting to kick in, you can challenge it by telling yourself and/or asking yourself the following:

- My anxiety has its origins in the past—at a time when I did not feel secure and was vulnerable. It is only partly related to anything going on now, but it amplifies any anxiety that I may be legitimately experiencing.

- How truly vulnerable am I, now, today, in this situation? What's the worst thing that could happen?

- What can I do, now, to make myself feel secure and safe, that I could not do in the past?

- Who truly loves and cares about me now? Who can I trust to be there for me if and when I need them?

- Am I better able to defend myself today than I may have been in the past?

- What resources do I have today that I can turn to in order to feel safe and secure?

In Brent's case the new assignment that the college had given him could be expected to be a reasonable source of at least some anxiety, as it would be to anyone who found himself in that position. However, that "legitimate" anxiety was vastly amplified by his insecurity, which raised it to the level of an almost paralyzing free-floating anxiety. That insight alone, he told me, provided him with some relief. "If I think of that free-floating anxiety as a sort of ghost from the past," he explained, "it sort of loses some of its power, as I realize that I'm living in the present, and I'm not that frail, vulnerable boy who had no resources to turn to. Sometimes it even helps if I look at myself in the mirror and see that there is no small boy there. Then I realize that I've been walking around for years acting as if I was that boy."

Brent also used the other questions cited to challenge his free-floating anxiety, and over time he made good progress with it. In addition, we looked at other ways that have been found useful in combating free-floating anxiety.

MEDITATION

The problem with anxiety is that it fogs our thinking and can prevent us from perceiving a situation clearly and accurately. That's because of the way our bodies are hard-wired. When we are anxious, we become vigilant for a threat. Even when an objective, external threat is not apparent, our perception can be distorted. If you doubt that, try having a rational conversation with someone when they are feeling very anxious. It's very difficult.

Reducing anxiety has the advantage of allowing a person to think more clearly and evaluate a situation more accurately. When anxiety is decreased we are in a better position to sort out reality from fantasy. We are then in a position to identify whatever it is that is bothering us, irritating us, or making us anxious. In turn, we can pause to contemplate how we might address these issues appropriately instead of blowing up in anger, making false accusations, or otherwise damaging a relationship. In Brent's case, as just described, reducing his free-floating anxiety also allowed him to be more "present" when he was with his wife and daughters.

One technique for managing anxiety and stress is called mindfulness-based stress reduction. It has its origins in research that sought to help people cope with chronic pain, with minimal or no added pain medication. Although necessary in some cases, these medications are best used on an acute, time-limited basis. Used long-term, pain medications can lose their effectiveness, and many are also addicting. The same is true for most antianxiety medications; over time they lose their effectiveness and are addicting.

As an adjunct to medications, researchers have experimented with a variety of alternative treatments. The method described here, mindfulness meditation, has been found to be effective in reducing pain as well as stress levels. It can therefore be a valuable tool for men looking to manage or overcome MBPD.

Mindfulness meditation is best practiced once a day for twenty minutes or so. In order for it to be effective you must find a place where you can be comfortable and where the surroundings are quiet for at least that long. Here is what to do:

- Make sure the clothes you are wearing are comfortable and the room you are in is comfortable as well—no glaring lights or loud background noises, not too hot or cold.

- Try to make sure you will not be interrupted for at least twenty minutes.

- Set a timer (preferably one with a gentle ring) for half an hour (in case you fall asleep).

- Find a comfortable place to lie down—flat, on your back if possible. You may also sit in a chair or on a cushion in a position that allows you to keep your spine straight and your head and neck supported and aligned with your spine without strain.

- Close your eyes and focus your attention on your own breathing. Feel the air go in, and then out of your lungs. Breathe naturally; don't try to increase or decrease the rate at which you breathe.

- Allow any outside noises to just pass over you while keeping your attention on your breathing; breathe in and out fully and naturally from your diaphragm, following each of your incoming and outgoing breaths.

- Allow any thoughts you may have to also pass in and then out of your mind. Do not get stuck on any one thought; just let the thoughts flow in and out of your consciousness with each breath.

- Allow any other body sensations, including pain or anxiety, to flow in and out of your body. Do not focus on such feelings; rather, let them pass over, through, and out of you, just like a gentle wave would pass over you if you were standing in the sea.

Practicing the above routine on a daily basis will have a cumulative effect on your stress and anxiety levels; in other words, the longer you practice mindfulness meditation the less overall stress or anxiety you will feel. That reduction in and of itself can lead to a decrease in your tendency to experience free-floating anxiety. It can also help you to think more clearly and, like Brent, to be more "present" in your relationships.

OTHER METHODS

Mindfulness meditation is one technique that has been found to effectively reduce stress and anxiety (and pain). There are others. A technique called Transcendental Meditation (TM) asks the individual to focus not so much on his or her breathing, but on a word or image, called a mantra. As with mindfulness meditation, research has documented TM's positive effects.

Yoga is also effective at reducing stress. Unlike meditation, which can be self-taught, yoga is best learned through instruction. Introductory yoga classes are fairly popular and relatively inexpensive, and should not be too difficult to locate. Brent, in fact, chose yoga over meditation, as he had a couple of colleagues at the college who'd been practicing it for years and swore by it.

Finally, massage is an effective stress-reducer. However, it can be the most costly option. Therapeutic massage may be covered under some health insurance policies, though there may be limitations on the number of sessions allowed. There are also massage schools, which offer lower rates than established practices.

CONSISTENCY

The National Center for Complementary and Alternative Medicine (nccam.nih.gov) is a useful resource that provides information on all of the above methods, as well as others. It also provides users with links so that they can read about the research supporting the effectiveness of these methods. One thing that all of this research supports is the notion that, to be truly effective, a person needs to pursue one of these methods consistently. They are all effective; therefore, the task facing you is to choose one and then stick with it. As an example, consider yoga. When one group of people who attended eight yoga classes was compared to a second group who had been practicing yoga once a week for two years, it was found that both groups had reduced stress levels, but the second group had a significantly greater reduction in stress.

So, if you decide to try meditating, but you only meditate once a week for three weeks, don't expect a significant reduction in your stress or anxiety levels. On the other hand, if you practice meditation five or six times a week for several weeks, you should begin to notice an effect. Not that meditating is a cure for Borderline Personality Disorder. But the fact is that free-floating anxiety plagues many men with MBPD. It clouds their thinking, often leading them to make false conclusions (for example, that a loved one is rejecting them when that is not the case). By learning a technique that has been found to reduce stress and practicing it consistently, men with MBPD can put themselves in a position to cope more effectively with other issues such as insecurity.

SUMMING UP

Because free-floating anxiety is so common among those with MBPD I chose to begin this "solutions" part of the book by addressing it first. Free-floating anxiety is linked to insecurity, though most men with BPD are not consciously aware of that connection. Free-floating anxiety can be attacked in two ways, beginning by "connecting the dots" between it and the inner insecurity that drives it. Men can use insight, combined with a technique for taking stock and confronting their anxiety, to question the "legitimacy" of the anxiety they are feeling. How much of it is based in current reality, versus the portion of it that is just a ghost from the past?

Men can also learn to reduce free-floating anxiety by learning and consistently practicing one of the methods described in this chapter. By doing so they will find that they are better able to "stop and think" as opposed to reacting impulsively based on a false perception.

CHAPTER SEVEN

Finding Your Voice

We've already seen that much of the behavior associated with Borderline Personality Disorder operates on an unconscious level. For example, insecurity that is rooted in early experiences of rejection, abuse, or abandonment is typically not connected in the mind of the MBPD man with behaviors such as

- Being thin-skinned: Hypervigilant for rejection, and quick to feel hurt and/or anger.

- Being self-destructive: Driven by self-hatred, feeling that he is either "second best" or "damaged goods."

- Experiencing free-floating anxiety: A nagging feeling of dread.

- Being moody: Easily slipping into depression and/or having a hair-trigger temper.

- Substance abuse: turning to alcohol or other drugs to cope with negative feelings such as anxiety or depression.

The man with BPD just doesn't "connect the dots" between early experiences and his behavior as an adult. One reason is that those experiences may have occurred long ago and are largely forgotten. Research has shown, for example, that we are inclined to hold on to positive memories and forget negative ones that can cause us discomfort. In other words, human beings are susceptible to nostalgia. In cases of severe trauma we may experience periodic flashbacks for a long time. Much of the rejection, abandonment, and/or abuse that lead to insecurity and eventually to MBPD, however, is not so severe as to be traumatic. This is true in particular for people with mild to moderate MBPD. The bottom line, then, is that they are apt to forget those negative experiences over time and therefore fail to see the connection between those experiences and their current behavior.

Men with BPD are not a different species from men who do not have BPD. All men are capable of experiencing insecurity and free-floating anxiety. All men are capable of feeling jealous and of being defensive at times. The difference for men with BPD is that the deep insecurity associated with MBPD leads these men to be hypervigilant and hypersensitive. Their MBPD serves as an amplifier, causing their emotional responses to be more intense. So a slight criticism or complaint from a loved one that might simply get a non-MBPD man's attention and make him momentarily uncomfortable, can cause the man with MBPD to explode in rage, to fall into a deep depression, or to self-medicate with substances.

In order to break the above cycle the man with MBPD must learn to correct his perceptions. In effect, he needs to be able to turn his "emotional amplifier" off so that he can react to interactions as they are, as opposed to reacting on the basis of exaggerated feelings of rejection or abandonment. This is not easy, and the man with MBPD should expect to make slow progress as opposed to changing dramatically and quickly. On the other hand, progress is possible for the MBPD man who sets that as a goal. The potential rewards are significant: less anxiety, fewer hurt feelings, more satisfying relationships, and self-acceptance as opposed to self-hatred.

First Step: Putting Words to Feelings

Learning to turn off your emotional amplifier involves two steps and the first of these is learning to put feelings into words. Men with BPD often act as if they are intensely angry, yet if asked they will not realize they are in fact angry. Similarly, they are often unable to name free-floating anxiety for what it is, or say that they are feeling the pain associated with abandonment or rejection. If you suggest that they are feeling abandoned or rejected they may get defensive and deny it, as obvious as it seems. Lacking that insight they are therefore at a loss as to what to do about such feelings so as to make themselves feel calmer and more secure.

Interestingly, men with BPD may not be hypersensitive and defensive in all situations; rather, it is in the context of their most intimate relationships that their emotional amplifier emerges. Here is an example:

Gary had decided to commit to counseling after quitting drinking for a period of six months. He had turned to a twelve-step program for support and despite his initial skepticism he'd found what he described as a "home" there. "I had the usual hesitation at first," he explained. "Like many other people, I suppose, I thought I'd find a bunch of burnouts and losers at twelve-step meetings. Boy was I surprised! I found a couple of men's meetings and quickly discovered that these guys weren't losers at all. In fact, a number of them were professionals like me."

Gary was a Certified Public Accountant (CPA) who worked for a law firm. His specialties included taxes and estate planning. He would work with one of the two lawyers in the firm who also specialized in those areas, helping mostly upper-middle-class individuals and couples plan ahead. Divorced, Gary had no children and had been in his current relationship for two years. It was partly due to pressure from his girlfriend, Rita, that Gary decided to rethink his drinking. He concluded that he was no longer the occasional "social" drinker that he once was, and that he wanted to quit, at least for a while. "I wasn't thinking about quitting forever," he said. "But after being abstinent for a couple of months I felt so much better that I decided not to go back."

It was also Rita who had suggested that Gary give a twelve-step program a try. She had two good friends, she'd said, who believed that a twelve-step program had transformed their lives. So although Gary was not at all convinced he was addicted to alcohol, he decided to give the Twelve Steps a try. "I knew I could use some support in quitting," he said, "even if I wasn't a full-fledged addict."

In truth, when he came for counseling, Gary still was not convinced that he was ever "dependent" on drinking, though he had no doubt that the comfort, support, and "love" he found in his twelve-step program had made a big difference in his life. More than that, he'd come to realize that in many ways he'd sought that same comfort from drinking. "What surprised me most," he told me, "was how accepting and supportive these people were. I think I expected them to be judgmental. One time, when I went to a meeting and said that I'd had a few drinks the night before after arguing with Rita, I half-expected the group to kick me out. I was shocked, frankly, when they welcomed me with open arms. That one experience sealed the deal for me. With or without a label, I consider myself a member of my twelve-step program. I attend two meetings a week, including my home group meeting, and I have a sponsor I talk to or email several times a week."

Gary's expectation that he would be rejected (and abandoned) by the twelve-step program because he'd had a few drinks was part and parcel of his MBPD. He readily admitted that he was "thin-skinned" and that this had been a problem for him in all his relationships. "I'm not confident in myself at all," he explained. "On some level I just don't seem to believe that I'm smart enough, or good looking enough, or funny enough, to keep a woman. I expect to be rejected, and I can sink into a depression at the drop of a hat."

I asked Gary if he was the same way at work as he was in his relationships. He laughed. "Not at all!" he replied. "At work I know I come across as confident, because I am. If someone has a question about some figures or projections I've come up with I have no problem explaining it. I never doubt myself. But in my relationships it's totally different."

Gary was dealing with some severe insecurity, though he did not recognize or label it as such. Rather than trying to put words to his feelings, when he was hurt he would withdraw into himself and become sullen. Rita had witnessed this many times, and she attributed it to Gary being very "defensive" and "sensitive" to use her words.

It was only after we spent some time talking about Gary's formative years that a picture began to emerge of where the origins of his MBPD lay. At first, Gary said he had very little recollection of those years. To facilitate our discussion I asked him if he possessed a family photo album or had some other way of gaining access to pictures of himself and his family as he was growing up. Many men with MBPD have only sparse memories of their childhoods. While almost everyone has an imperfect memory, I believe this is even more so for those with MBPD. I suspect that is because these people have a desire to suppress those memories. Going through old photos is one way to help unlock those memories and get a picture of what it was like to be that person growing up.

As it turned out Gary did not have a family photo album, but his sister did and she was willing to lend it to him. I asked Gary to take some time to look through the album before we talked about it. He did so, with Rita, and the next time he came to see me we had a very fruitful discussion. Here is what Gary said:

"As a child, beginning when I was about ten, I put on a lot of weight—so much so that the pediatrician had diagnosed me as obese and advised my mother to restrict my food intake, especially snacks. She did nothing of the kind. Rather, she seemed determined to keep me fat. She was quite overweight herself, as was my sister. Naturally I got picked on in school. I was terrible at sports. The class I hated most was gym—the class that all the other boys liked the best!

"I'm the only one in my family who ever lost that weight, starting in high school. It might be hard to believe, but I actually got criticized for that at home—for not eating enough.

"I can only remember one time when my father hit me, and I remember that afterward he came to my room and said he was sorry. My mother, though, slapped me often. My father never did anything about that.

"My mother always said that I was a difficult child, but I don't know in what way I was difficult. She complained many times that as an infant I was colicky and kept her awake all night. How was I responsible for that? I was an infant. But to listen to her you'd think I did it on purpose.

"Growing up it was always clear to me that my sister was my mother's favorite, and I never could figure why that was, *either. I remember one Christmas when she got at least three times the gifts I did. When I asked my mother how come Marie got so many more presents, my mother just laughed and said, 'Because I love her more.' She said it like she was making a joke. Only it wasn't a joke to me."*

Gary, who as an adult man was trim and fit, said that he did not like visiting his parents. When he told them he was getting a divorce, his mother had said something like, "Well, I was more or less expecting that. You never were the easiest person to live with." And after he introduced Rita to the family, Gary's mother had remarked, "I'm so glad you've found someone who can accept you as you are." As a therapist, just hearing Gary say that made my back stiffen, as I imagined what it would be like to hear my own mother say that to me.

Over the past couple of years Gary had visited with his family only out of a sense of obligation, and only on holidays. His mother would complain at times that he came by so rarely, but I could understand why.

Some would say that Gary's upbringing was not traumatic, and that might be true. However, it's also true that his formative years did not foster security or self-confidence. When I asked Gary if he could relate to the words "second best" or "damaged goods" he nodded firmly. "Yes, second best—that was me."

Gary's story, while unique to him, nevertheless struck a theme that has become familiar for me in my work with BPD men. He grew up feeling second best—not good enough. His formative relationships with his mother and father had not promoted a sense of security and of being valued. When I asked him if he felt that he could turn to his family or rely on them "when the chips are down" he frowned and shook his head. "No way," he said, "I'd never count on them."

In his career Gary functioned at a high level; but his relationships were another matter. He was jealous and insecure — frequently harboring thoughts that Rita would leave him. He was very uncomfortable when she would dress in clothing that, from his point of view, emphasized her nice figure and made her look sexy. He did not like it when she would meet girlfriends for a drink at Friday happy hours once a month. If they had a disagreement he would fall into a depression. He would avoid even the slightest conflict, only to sulk about it. On those few occasions when Rita had said she wasn't up for it when he suggested sex, he'd find himself mulling over it the whole next day. And so on.

In order to break out of this cycle, which he knew was slowly but surely driving Rita away, Gary needed to give a voice to his insecurity. Up until now, though, he hadn't even been able to name either insecurity or free-floating anxiety or have any clue as to why he experienced these feelings. So as a preliminary step we spent some time learning to put feelings into words, and connecting those feelings to their root cause.

The place we started in helping Gary to find his voice was with his parents. When I would ask Gary how he felt as he was describing his experiences as a child—for example, when his mother seemingly tried to keep him obese—he would get visibly uncomfortable. "Does it make you angry?" I asked. Again he squirmed; then he nodded. "Yeah it does, but then I don't feel right about that. It's like it isn't right to be angry at her." I then asked, "Could that be in part because your mother had you convinced, as a child, that it was always your fault?" Gary nodded. "Bingo!" he replied.

Like many of the men I've worked with, Gary had trouble putting a name to his feelings. It was, of course, no surprise that he would feel angry at his mother for favoring his sister and putting him down, and angry at his father as well for never sticking up for him. But Gary would feel guilty if he admitted to such feelings. Indeed, his mother had systematically encouraged that guilt for years by complaining about what a difficult child Gary had been. As best I could tell nothing could have been further from the truth, but like all children he naïvely believed what his mother said and assumed that he was at fault whenever she would criticize him or hit him.

It took a while for Gary to get comfortable with the fact that he was angry and to put a name to that feeling when it was associated with certain memories. From anger we moved to anxiety. For Gary, as for many MBPD men, that anxiety reflected the insecurity he'd long known. Feeling "second best" (even if you don't use those words to describe it) does not make a person feel valuable or desirable. On the contrary, it would lead him or her to the belief (again, perhaps not consciously) that he or she could be discarded the moment something better came along. That was exactly how Gary had always felt in relationships. In time, he was able to put a name to that feeling as well.

From Thoughts to Words

About a month later Gary told me about a phone call he'd gotten from his mother. She'd called to invite him to come over to celebrate her birthday. He did not like visiting his parents, but once more he felt obligated to accept the invitation. "She also told me to bring Rita," Gary said. "Then she said something like 'I hope you're treating her well.' And I said, 'Of course I'm treating her well! It makes me angry that you would even imply that I was not.'"

That was a breakthrough for Gary. I asked him how his mother had reacted. He said she seemed flustered; then she denied that she'd made any such implication, which brought Gary to a critical crossroad. Was he going to believe his mother, and therefore feel guilty about getting angry; or, was he going to trust his own gut reaction?

In the past, Gary acknowledged, he'd always abandoned his own gut reaction. "That's why you have trouble putting a name to your anger and legitimizing it," I told him. "But your reaction to what your mother said was right on. It was a put-down. From now on you need to pause before you abandon your gut feelings, because a lot of the time those feelings are probably appropriate."

Finding your voice involves the same steps that Gary went through. Again, these are as follows:

STEP ONE: GIVE A NAME TO YOUR FEELINGS

Men are not, generally speaking, socialized to articulate their feelings very well. Just as women are more likely to describe a particular color in a more complex way ("It's sort of a soft silvery blue."), men tend to oversimplify ("It's blue."). The same is true for emotions. That's okay. A woman might be able to name her feeling as "mildly annoyed," whereas a man—one who was able to recognize his feelings, that is—might simply say, "I'm mad."

Subtlety and complexity can be nice, but putting a name to your feelings is what is critical here. Emotions that men with Borderline Personality Disorder have the hardest time putting a name to include anger, anxiety, envy, and jealousy. A husband who is insecure, for example, may feel anxious when his wife dresses up for a social occasion. He may or may not be consciously aware that he is jealous of every other man in the room and is vigilant in observing those men for any signs of flirtation on the part of his wife. He may have a miserable time, and may brood through the entire evening. Chances are his wife will be aware of his sour mood, but not necessarily its cause, especially if she knows for sure that she was not being flirtatious. He may drink too much, and on the drive home he may snap when his wife asks him what was wrong that night.

What is going on inside this man is that his insecurity is generating free-floating anxiety. He is uncomfortable and uneasy about the evening, but he has no idea why. In other words, he cannot connect his anxiety to his fear of abandonment. In fact, if someone suggested that to him, he might even laugh it off. After all, he is a man. He is *not* insecure. He is tough! Underneath that exterior, though, is a lingering feeling that he is not good enough, that his wife can't be trusted, or both.

The real breakthrough for those with MBPD is to realize and accept the fact that they are in fact sensitive, and most likely have been wounded as a consequence of abandonment, rejection, and/or abuse. Perhaps that abuse was dramatic and obvious; or, as was true for Gary, it may have taken a somewhat more subtle form. The difference may be reflected to some extent in the intensity of a man's BPD, which as we've discussed can vary from relatively mild to very severe.

STEP TWO: GIVE A VOICE TO YOUR FEELINGS

It is no easy task for the MBPD man to learn to articulate how he is feeling, and then to accept it. He may hesitate because he is ashamed to admit he feels, for example, jealous or insecure. Or, like Gary, he may feel guilty about being angry. Such emotions stand in the way of accepting what he feels, and then legitimizing it. "Is it okay to feel jealous of other men, and insecure about my wife's commitment to me?" "Is it okay to feel angry at my parent(s)?"

Just as it can be an internal struggle to name and accept feelings, it can take significant courage to give a voice to them. Of course, sometimes this happens more or less spontaneously, as it did when Gary's mother made that snide comment during their phone call. Even then, however, it can be unsettling. Gary surprised himself when he expressed anger at his mother's implied criticism, and when she denied it he hesitated for a moment, almost taking it back. It was good for him that he didn't back away, and it marked a turning point not only in his relationship with his parents, but also in his relationship with Rita. This did not happen overnight. Rather, it was a process in which Gary gradually learned to identify his feelings and give a voice to them.

In time, Gary was able to name it when he was experiencing free-floating anxiety. He could see how that anxiety might have some cause in the present, but also how it was being amplified by his insecurity. He was also able to appreciate how it could distort his perceptions and lead to false conclusions. For instance, if Rita and he had a minor disagreement he might initially feel a little upset—but that minor upset would be amplified into major anxiety by the insecurity that was rooted in his belief that he'd always been "second best" and basically a person who was difficult to live with, as his mother had often repeated. He'd then begin to imagine that Rita was thinking of leaving him. Without this insight—as to where his insecurity came from and how it affected his perceptions and emotional reactions—Gary would have been tempted to drink, or he might have blown up in anger. Neither of these alternatives would have improved his self-confidence or helped relieve his borderline personality, and both would have been destructive to his relationship with Rita.

Easy Does It

The kind of changes I have been discussing in this chapter take time. A man does not develop a borderline personality overnight; consequently he does not leave it behind overnight. If you recognize MBPD in yourself, you might consider asking a loved one to assist you in this process; or, you might enlist the aid of a therapist. The task is simple enough in one way: learn to identify your feelings and then express them so that they can be addressed. For example, when Gary was able to identify and communicate his anxiety and insecurity to Rita they were able to talk about it. She could understand his jealousy, for example, as jealousy is an emotion that virtually everyone can identify with. At the same time, having his jealousy out in the open allowed Gary and Rita to acknowledge and talk about it. For her part she voluntarily made sure that she paid attention to Gary and complimented him. She didn't have to give him all her attention, or make up reasons to compliment him, because she genuinely enjoyed his company and admired him. She just took a little extra time to make sure he knew this as well.

For his part Gary was able to name his demons and then confront them. He could see how his insecurity got its start, and how it affected him. From that starting point he was able to challenge his insecurity, in part by asking himself the kinds of questions outlined in the last chapter. Two questions in particular that he learned to ask himself often were:

- Am I "second best"?
- Am I difficult to live with?

When last we met, Gary struck me as remarkably relaxed and I said so. The stress lines that so often had furrowed his brow were gone. I told him he looked good. "I am good," he said. "I think I am on a good track now. I still have my moments. I've learned to tell myself that I'm no longer that obese boy who lived with a mother who treated him as second best. I'm a successful, physically fit man who has a relationship with a wonderful woman who appreciates me for all I have to offer."

SUMMING UP

Learning to moderate free-floating anxiety—the subject of the last chapter—can help set the stage for learning to find your voice. It's common for men with BPD to avoid or even deny their feelings. Once more this may reflect our cultural stereotype in which being "sensitive" is not considered manly. Rather, men are expected to emulate NFL linebackers, both physically and emotionally. Aggressiveness and competitiveness are fine, sensitivity and anxiety are not. Unfortunately, buying into this stereotype becomes a trap, and not just for the man with BPD. By learning to put their feelings into words, and then giving those feelings a voice, men can start down the pathway to improved self-esteem, better relationships, and peace of mind.

CHAPTER EIGHT

Facing the Demon Within: Living with Insecurity

Most of us like to believe that as we were growing up, at least one of our parents loved us without reservation. We may be able to accept (perhaps reluctantly) the notion that one parent may have had a favored child and that we were not that child. We may compensate for that with the belief that we were favored by our other parent. At the very least we may take solace in the thought that while we were not the favored one, we were nevertheless loved.

What would it be like growing up as a boy whose parent (or parents) behaved in ways and communicated in ways that suggested they were either not sure they loved him, or definitely did not love him? How would that boy be likely to react? What kind of self-concept would evolve for that boy? And, finally, how would that boy approach relationships as an adult?

The Roots of Insecurity: Rejection, Abandonment, and Ambivalence

Children have a remarkable ability to read their parents' emotions. As an example, consider what happens when a parent, who is carrying an infant, encounters a person the parent (but not the infant) knows. The first thing the infant does is glance at the parent's facial expression. If that expression shows discomfort, the infant is apt to squirm, or even cry, and will usually bury his or her face. On the other hand, if the parent's face expresses warmth (or at least not stress), then the infant will be comfortable and may even smile at the stranger.

Born with that kind of "emotional radar" it is little wonder that children can "read" their parents' emotions and interpret them as friendly or hostile, accepting or rejecting, loving or unloving. The same applies to children's ability to read and interpret their parents' body language, words, and actions. Though he may never actually put into words, a boy knows from the way a parent looks at him, talks to him, and touches him whether that parent is loving, accepting, rejecting, or ambivalent about him. And he can read this even when his parent is not aware of it.

Children instinctively seek the security of knowing that they are loved unconditionally. That's not to say that a parent never gets angry at them, but what it does mean is that the anger will pass and the unreserved love will return.

In some respects outright hostility and rejection from a parent may be easier for a child to cope with than a parent's ambivalence. If we know someone does not like us (even if we do not know why) we have a choice: either we try to win over that person and gain his or her approval, or we can look elsewhere for it. I have known men and women who opted for the second alternative as children. Faced with a hostile parent or step-parent, a boy may try for a while to turn that relationship around. However, faced with steadfast rejection, he will most often look to another relationship, for example, with a grandparent, uncle or aunt, or even an older sibling. We have also known boys who, being either fatherless or faced with a rejecting father, have turned to coaches or teachers for that approving and comforting connection. A good coach-player bond is not unlike a good father-son bond. The coach sets expectations for the players but also provides guidance. And the youth knows he can count on the coach when the chips are down. The same is true of a loving father.

Faced with an ambivalent parent (or parents), a boy finds himself in an altogether different situation. He perceives that sometimes the parent seems to like him and can be nurturing and supportive. But that is not to be counted on, because the parent can change and become unsupportive and rejecting, or even abusive. Gary, who was described in the last chapter, had an ambivalent mother, as did Luke, who described his formative years this way:

> "What I remember most about my father, as I was growing up, was that most of the time he was not there. He was a long-distance truck driver. He'd bought his own rig and he made good money hauling loads cross-country. I never heard him complain about it so I assumed he liked it. He was kind of an adventurous man who couldn't sit still for long. He would be gone for weeks at a time. I'd miss him. Sometimes I'd even have imaginary conversations with him. And then one day I'd get off the school bus and see his cab parked off to the side of the driveway. It was a rich royal blue,

and my father always kept it spotless, the chrome gleaming. It had a sleeping compartment, and my father would let me spend time in there, reading a book or drawing.

"Dad could be home anywhere from a day to a week. If it was more than a couple of days, though, he'd usually go off fishing. If it was a weekend I'd go with him. I really loved my father, and I know he loved me. He just had that wanderlust and got antsy being at home.

"I'm not sure what kind of marriage my parents had, but I can't imagine it could have been much since my father was home so little. Yet I can't remember my mother complaining, either. She and her sister had been raised by my grandmother and a great aunt after my grandfather had abandoned his family when my mother was still a baby. So she grew up without a man around, and maybe she liked it that way as a wife, too.

"My mother definitely favored my sister over me. Looking back on it, that could also have had something to do with her not having much experience relating to males. Anyway, it seemed that nothing I could do would be enough to please my mother. And believe me, I tried.

"There were times when my mother would be nice to me—but I really had to work for it. For example, if I tried cleaning my room when she asked me to she would always find ten items wrong when she came in to inspect it. Of course she never told me to do these things differently to begin with, so how was I to know? If I fought with my sister it would always be me who got the punishment. I really was

not a bad kid, but in my mother's eyes it was as if I was always falling just a bit short.

"The thing that hurt the most, though, was seeing how affectionate my mother could be with my sister, but how she would run hot and cold with me. I could never be sure if she would return my effort to hug her, or turn me away. If I got hurt I couldn't be sure if she would comfort me and bandage my injury, or scold me for acting in an irresponsible way."

Luke's mother's words and actions spoke loudly about her ambivalence. We can't tell if it was Luke himself she had mixed feelings about, or whether she was uncomfortable about being the mother of a son. Either way, the message was the same: I have mixed feelings about you.

Luke was also one of those boys who suffered from what I call "father hunger." He loved his father, but the man was seldom available. Theirs was not a bad relationship so much as one that left young Luke hungry for more. He did not really want a substitute; what he craved was more from his father. And again, though he did not name it as such, Luke had felt repeatedly abandoned by his father.

Luke responded to his mother's ambivalence in a way that I've seen often in the backgrounds of those with MBPD. Specifically, because he wasn't rejected outright he worked hard to win his mother's approval, nurturance, and affection. When he did not get it he would blame himself for not meeting expectations, in other words for not being "good enough" (as opposed to seeing his mother's ambivalence for what it was).

Growing up, Luke did experience periodic bouts of free-floating anxiety that stem from insecurity and are part and parcel of Borderline Personality Disorder. As an adolescent he'd been exceptionally moody, and among his peers he had a reputation for being smart but sarcastic. A female friend had once remarked that Luke was overly judgmental. What she meant, she explained, was that Luke seemed to be always on the lookout for people letting him down. Even the slightest broken promise—for example, making a date and then having to cancel it—could generate a spate of nasty criticism from him. He readily agreed when I asked him if the phrase "thin-skinned" described him accurately.

Was Luke's MBPD severe? Not as severe as some other MBPD clients I've worked with. But it was there, and it definitely took a toll on his quality of life. His mother was not overtly abusive; in fact, she may never have been consciously aware of her own ambivalence. Nevertheless, Luke had lived with it for years. And would Luke's father have entertained the idea that he'd abandoned his son? Doubtful, as from his point of view he was simply doing what he needed to do to support his family. Yet from young Luke's point of view that's what it felt like as his father would disappear for weeks at a time, time and time again.

Luke was now thirty, and had recently gotten engaged for the second time when he came to see me. His first fiancée had broken off their engagement a month before they were scheduled to be married. Luke had come to accept that this had been mostly his fault. "I think she just got worn down by my being thin-skinned and by my sarcasm," he explained.

As Luke described that first engagement it became clear that his insecurity had eventually pushed his fiancée to her limit. He was always feeling offended, he said, as a consequence of some little thing she did or said. "Half the time she'd claim she wasn't even aware of doing what I was accusing her of doing. At the time I thought she was lying about that, but I've come to believe it was probably true."

The other thing that had eventually killed Luke's first engagement was his insecurity and constant need for reassurance. His fiancée had been a mid-level manager who had to travel about once a month on business. Luke hated it when she went away. He'd feel anxious the whole time. He'd call, email, and/or text her many times a day. When they spoke he'd complain about feeling depressed. He knew he came across as weak and whining, but he couldn't seem to stop himself.

In the end that woman had explained that she believed Luke loved her, and that he had many qualities and attributes that she was looking for and admired. That said, she did not believe that she could be happy, over the long run, with Luke's neediness, his excessive sensitivity, and the biting sarcasm that surfaced whenever he was hurt or upset—which seemed to be often. She'd returned his ring, and given him a final hug, and then she was gone, literally, for a vacation with two female friends.

Luke was open enough to acknowledge the role he'd played in the breakup, and to understand that he would need to change if he hoped to have the life he envisioned for himself, which included marriage and a close family life—the very kind of family life he'd yearned for as a boy. Like the vast majority of men in his situation, though, he did not label his "symptoms," including his free-floating anxiety, hypersensitivity, and need for reassurance as insecurity, much less see them as aspects of his Borderline Personality Disorder. Similarly, he had never "connected the dots" between his adult personality and temperament and his experiences growing up. Naturally, he was therefore at a loss as to what to do.

Living with Insecurity

You read that right—*living* with insecurity.

As much as Luke (and millions of others) might wish they could simply cast off their insecurity and move on, the reality is that a more realistic goal is to acknowledge that it exists, recognize where it is coming from, and then learn ways to mitigate it so that it does not make you miserable or contaminate your relationships. Following this approach, many men will find that over time they are able to tame their insecurity, if not cast it off entirely. In time it can be reduced from a demon that dominates and controls their lives to a small beast that may rear its head from time to time, but which never takes control.

What follows is a technique that Luke and many other men have found useful.

NAME YOUR SYMPTOMS

In order to control the demon that is insecurity you first need to be able to name it. In the classic film *The Exorcist*, the priest who is brought in to conduct the exorcism begins to cure the possessed teenager by asking the demon to name itself. So it is, in a way, with insecurity. Some of the most prominent symptoms associated with it (its "names") are

- Free-floating anxiety: Feeling anxious but not being exactly sure why. Or, a vague feeling of dread that something bad might happen, though you are not sure what.

- Thin-skinned: Being hypervigilant for being abandoned, abused, or rejected by others. This can lead to anger or depression.

- Seeking reassurance: Feeling a need to be told that you are loved or seeking that reassurance through attention or affection.

Luke could identify with all of the above, and he was able to begin the task of living with his insecurity when he was able to pause for a second and put a name to what he was doing or feeling. For example, whenever his second fiancée, Anise, would meet a friend to do some shopping, or meet a couple of friends for a drink after work, Luke would experience the same discomfort he had when his first fiancée had done those activities. He tried to suppress those feelings, sometimes with more success than others. Even if he resisted calling or texting Anise on those occasions, he found himself feeling depressed. His preference, he admitted, would be for him and Anise to do everything together. Similarly, whenever Anise would have to be away overnight for a business meeting (she was a regional sales manager), he would seek reassurance by contacting her and telling her how much he missed her, waiting for her to say something comforting in response.

Luke was able to admit that his complaints, whenever Anise had to travel (or sometimes even work late), were most likely an effort to get her to feel guilty, reassure him, and perhaps even to return to be with him. Of course, cutting short a business trip was not an option, and Anise said that she believed Luke went "over the top" with his multiple calls, emails, and messages at those times.

Luke would experience this same discomfort if he sensed that Anise was even the least bit annoyed with him. He knew, for example, that his sarcasm irritated her at times (as it had irritated many people in his life), but once again Luke felt unable to stifle it.

Change began for Luke when he was able to recognize and name his discomfort, as well as the behaviors it provoked. Whereas Luke would once have acted on this discomfort—typically by seeking reassurance or being sarcastic—he learned to put a name to his demon: insecurity. He was able to learn to tell himself that he was experiencing free-floating anxiety. As mild as that may sound, its effects were actually quite dramatic. Without a name for the effects, Luke was at the mercy of his anxiety and insecurity; nor could he tame the sarcasm that stemmed from his insecurity. By beginning with a name, though, he now could face his demon and begin to do battle with it.

CONNECT THE DOTS

The next step that Luke was able to make, and this was another breakthrough, was to connect the dots and see the link between his current feelings and his experiences as a youth—particularly his absent father and his ambivalent mother. He would literally picture them in his mind, and it would then become immediately apparent that what he was currently feeling was being amplified by his insecurity. For example, it might be understandable that Luke would miss his fiancée if she went off shopping with friends for a day on the weekend or if she had to be away overnight. But his insecurity amplified that feeling and turned it into an intense free-floating anxiety. The insecure boy inside the adult Luke was reacting as if he were being rejected (by an ambivalent mother) and/or abandoned (by an absent father). Having Anise constantly at his side and being constantly reassured that she loved him (without a shred of ambivalence), were the only effective ways that could keep his insecurity at bay. Of course, these same needs on his part had already wrecked one potential marriage. If unchecked they could well deprive Luke of the future he envisioned for himself.

PLANT YOURSELF IN THE PRESENT AND FACE DOWN THE DEMON

The third step in the process that Luke learned to use was to "plant himself in the present" and then to "face down the demon." By that I meant that he needed to shift from the connection between his current feelings and their source in his past, to the reality of his current relationship with Anise. He could then challenge his insecurity by asking himself two questions:

- Am I really being abandoned by Anise?

- Is Anise really ambivalent about whether she loves me?

Luke could also ask himself the same questions when he felt hurt or angry in response to something a friend did or said:

- Is this friend really abandoning me?

- Is this friend really ambivalent about wanting this friendship?

Luke's insecurity, of course, did not just disappear. The demon was not exorcized simply by his trying out the above technique. It took some persistence on Luke's part in using the technique described above. On the other hand, it was remarkable just how well Luke was able to tame the demon over the long run and reduce it to proportions he could live with. As he described his insecurity six months later, "It used to be this big monster that could pop out at the drop of a hat and take me over. Now it's more like this pet dragon that I've learned to keep on a leash." At the same time he believed his relationship with Anise had grown stronger, and he felt confident that his chances for long-term happiness and a fulfilling family life were on the rise.

SUMMING UP

Insecurity is like a demon that lurks in the soul of the man with Borderline Personality Disorder. It sits there, always vigilant for the slightest sign of rejection or abandonment, and ready to spring forth. It brings with it a wave of free-floating anxiety; it invites the MBPD man to respond with anger, or to sink into depression. It can also tempt the MBPD man to "anesthetize" it through drinking alcohol or using other drugs.

Insecurity can be so very difficult to deal with because the man who is afflicted with it is often unable to name it for what it is, or connect it to its roots in that man's early experiences. His memory of those events that caused him to feel rejected or abandoned may have faded long ago, or he may not want to recall them. However, the ability to identify insecurity and connect it to its sources is crucial to being able to face it and reduce it over time. To do so transforms it from a demon that destroys relationships to a minor annoyance that can be kept within bounds.

CHAPTER NINE

From Self-Hatred to Self-Acceptance

One of the two core diagnostic criteria associated with Borderline Personality Disorder, in both men and women, is a dysfunctional, negative self-image. Such a self-image is dysfunctional because it denies the individual the opportunity to experience self-esteem. The person with BPD—no matter how talented, successful, or caring he or she may be—is unable to truly embrace that self-image. Instead, he or she is preoccupied with every fault, flaw, and failure, no matter how minor, that he or she may have. We all have such flaws. The healthy person is able to accept that, and in the best case work toward being the best person he or she can be. But for the person with BPD these normal flaws seem immense and insurmountable—so much so that they overshadow any good qualities or abilities the individual may possess.

Second Best and Damaged Goods

LIAM

Liam had recently turned twenty-one and had also just entered his senior year in college. He was an excellent student, but also one who'd spent his underclassman years living more on the fringes of college life than in its center. As a matter of fact he'd occupied that social position for as long as he could remember. He was clean-cut and trim; if a bit lacking in muscle tone. As a teen he'd been what you'd call lanky: tall and skinny and just a bit uncoordinated. He'd never had an interest in sports, either as a participant or an observer. He rarely drank, and preferred reading to playing video games. His taste in music tended toward jazz and classical more than rock, country, or metal. He was also shy. That combination of traits left him with slim pickings for a group of college peers to align with.

For a time in his high school years Liam had been a "cutter." He'd sit in his room late at night and scratch superficial wounds in his arms using a pocket knife. He'd never cut himself deeply enough to require anything more than a couple of band-aids, and his parents had never noticed anything (or if they did, they said nothing). He hadn't cut again since graduating high school — that is, until he started his senior year of college.

The major issue in Liam's life had to do with his father, Alec. The man was a gambling addict who'd more than once spent the family into severe debt. He could disappear for days at a time. Both Liam and his mother knew where they could find Alec — in one of two large casinos in the state — but they never bothered to try. After going on one of his gambling binges Alec would return to his job, which was as a salesman for office furniture. For this he drew a small weekly salary, and then earned commissions on his sales. It was usually after he'd earned a large commission that Alec was likely to disappear for a few days.

Liam's mother, Naomi, was as frustrated as her son was with Alec, but she was a devout Christian and would never consider divorce. So she studied and became a realtor and made a living that way. The problem with being a realtor, though, was that, like being a salesman, the income was not steady, and to some extent it was seasonal. So Naomi had to be able to make money stretch. Also, being a realtor meant that Naomi had to be available most nights and every weekend. She'd cook dinners and leave them in the fridge for Liam and Alec (that is, if Alec came home). Most nights Liam ate his meal in his room while reading, surfing Internet news sites, or listening to music.

The family had never been rich; and thanks to Alec's gambling it often had to make do with a sparse pantry and broken appliances. On two occasions the electricity had been cut off due to non-payment. Naomi bought most of Liam's clothes at secondhand shops, and though the items were clean and serviceable they were never the most stylish. And when it came time for Liam to go to college there was no money in the coffers, so Liam had to commute to school instead of living on campus, and needed to finance his education with loans.

Alec did very little around the house and Naomi had neither the time nor the energy to maintain household items, much less repair them when they broke. Liam tried to pick up a little of that slack; still, in many ways his home was in poor shape compared to those of the peers that he'd visited.

So that was life for Liam: his father's gambling binges continued unabated, and the family struggled by. The bottom line for Liam, of course, was that he'd never been able to rely on Alec, either as a provider or as a father. He could never rely on his father being home on any given night. He could never assume that there would be enough money for food the next week or for a fresh supply of consignment clothes for the coming school year.

Liam had few friends growing up, in large part because he was embarrassed about the relatively poor state of repair of his home and avoided bringing the few friends he had there. Liam was also embarrassed about his father, since quite a few people in their town and the church they attended knew about Alec's gambling problem and its effects on the family. Lastly, there was Liam's innate shyness, which caused him to hang back instead of engaging with others.

Liam was, on the plus side, smart, responsible, and somewhat creative. He liked to draw, and at times he tried his hand at writing, mostly short poems with a nature theme. He'd never indulged in drugs, and had never gotten into trouble with the law. His problem, then, centered around his social isolation and his poor self-esteem. According to Liam he was basically unattractive: too lanky and skinny, not athletic, too shy, and socially awkward. He was sure he was not attractive to girls. Consequently, he had never had a girlfriend and his social life had been limited to the rare party he'd be invited to. Even then he would fade into the background and leave early. Then he met Anna.

It was the end of Liam's junior college year. He'd done well, as usual, grade-wise, and had just started on the summer job in the supermarket where he'd worked every summer since his junior year in high school, mostly stocking shelves or packing items at one of the store's many check-out lanes. Anna had gotten a job as a cashier through a friend whose father was the store manager. She had also just finished her junior year and, like Liam, had set her sights on graduate school and a career as a special education teacher.

It was Anna who made the first move. Apparently, Liam was not as unattractive (or dreary) as he thought he was, for Anna approached him as he sat at a table in the small staff lounge during his daily half-hour lunch break. She said "hi," then, much to Liam's surprise, asked if she could join him. Thinking back on that first interaction, Liam could not recall if he actually spoke the word "yes" or simply nodded—he was that shocked!

So Anna sat down and struck up a conversation. It was as if she sensed Liam's shyness because she did most of the talking and made it easy by asking him some questions, mostly about college but also about where he lived, how long he'd been working at the supermarket, and so on. To say that Liam was excited would be a gross understatement, for he'd taken notice of Anna and thought she was very attractive.

After the break and their brief conversation ended, Liam ruminated about it, thinking he'd done a poor job of it. Needless to say he was pleasantly surprised when Anna sat down at the same table the next day—and then the day after that.

After a week of shared lunch breaks Anna invited Liam to a pool party at her house. Liam had been beside himself with anxiety ever since he accepted the invitation, though when he got to Anna's house he found the several friends who Anna had invited to be friendly and quite accepting of him. They talked mostly about college and what they were doing that summer, took frequent dips in the pool, and enjoyed a barbecue.

In many ways that day had been a pivotal experience for Liam, and he and Anna dated informally for the rest of that summer. They did not have sex (which was fine with Liam, who was extremely nervous about that) but they did kiss and cuddle while watching movies in Anna's family room. In time, Liam felt comfortable enough to share some of his drawings and poems with Anna.

As you might expect, Liam's experience that summer had the potential to trigger all of the insecurity that he'd held inside for so long. And sure enough it did. As soon as Liam returned to college for his senior year and Anna returned to her college, a two-hour drive away, Liam started cutting again.

Liam had never been the victim of outright abuse by either of his parents; neither had he been bullied very much. But there was no doubt, in his mind at least, that he was very much a "second best" person when it came to the social totem pole. That belief was what had driven him to become a cutter for a time in high school. As he described it, his self-hatred would build, and along with it his free-floating anxiety. He knew, of course, that other high school students were also cutters. Like him, they most likely also felt like second-best outcasts. Like him, they probably disliked themselves intensely. But because this group did not sit down and talk to one another, Liam was unaware of the likely commonalities between himself and this group of teens.

For reasons that were unclear even to him, Liam's cutting faded over the course of his senior year of high school, and then it had stopped altogether. Through college he'd managed his insecurity and free-floating anxiety primarily by devoting himself to his studies, to drawing and writing, and by listening to music. He also avoided close friendships. However, Anna had awakened the demon. More specifically, Liam's attraction to Anna had awakened his demon.

He found himself thinking about her all the time. Unfortunately, these thoughts were not always comforting. On the contrary, his thoughts often turned to worries that she would soon enough lose interest in him, or else be seduced by someone who had much more to offer than a young man with huge loans to repay, a father who was an unchecked gambling addict, and a home life that relied on his mother's ability to sell houses to save it from financial disaster. If Anna did not return his text messages promptly he would fret about it. And when she said she could not come home for a weekend visit because she had three tests the following Monday, Liam was sure that he was being dumped. It was in this context that Liam began cutting himself again—late at night, when he could get neither Anna herself, nor his worry that she would lose interest in him, out of his mind. It was on one of those lonely nights that Liam realized that he was deeply depressed, hated himself, and probably needed help.

WESLEY

Wesley shared Liam's low self-esteem and self-hatred, though for different reasons. Unlike Liam, Wesley had been the victim of abuse. His abuser had been an older stepbrother who had abused Wesley both physically and sexually for several years. The abuse began when Wesley had been about six, and ended only when the stepbrother moved out of the house. Wesley was nearly eleven by then.

Victims of sexual abuse are notorious for not disclosing their abuse, either to parents or police. This appears to be even more the case for boys. It's been hypothesized that boys do not disclose either sexual or physical abuse for the simple reason that being a victim runs counter to our cultural expectations for boys. In short, it isn't "manly" to be a victim. That was certainly true for Wesley, who actually was ashamed of himself for having been victimized.

Whereas Liam's self-hatred stemmed from his self-concept of being "second best," Wesley's self-hatred reflected a self-concept of being "damaged goods." Again, he was deeply ashamed of himself. In his case his self-hatred was reflected in alcohol and other drug abuse, conflict with authorities (especially teachers), as well as in his underachievement. Despite being tested and found to be highly intelligent, Wesley was a frequent truant and barely passed his courses. He was also both demanding and insecure in his relationships.

Unlike Liam, who avoided dating, Wesley, now twenty-one, had had a string of girlfriends beginning when he was fifteen, and those who he hadn't dumped had dumped him. He had been stifling in those relationships, demanding constant attention (while returning very little) and exploding in anger over the least disappointment or perceived rejection. He'd never been physically violent with his girlfriends; however, he could be incredibly cruel and verbally abusive.

Wesley did not seek out counseling willingly, as Liam did. What happened was that he got really drunk one night, after dismissing his latest girlfriend, and then staggered his way to a bridge that crossed a small river in the small town where he lived. A police officer spotted him from the cruiser where he'd been sitting, taking a break. The officer recognized Wesley, and he didn't like what he saw: Wesley climbing over the bridge railing. The officer rushed out of his cruiser and sneaked up on the drunk and oblivious Wesley, grabbing him around the chest and pulling him back from the brink.

Wesley spent several days in the psychiatric unit of a local hospital. It was then and there that he finally opened up and disclosed the truth about his past.

From Self-Hatred to Self-Acceptance

Both Liam and Wesley were burdened by the extreme sensitivity to perceived rejection that is a core component of the borderline personality and temperament. They may not have consciously been aware of believing that they were either second-best or damaged goods, but this attitude was very much reflected in their behavior.

The boy who is treated as if he were second-best or damaged goods will only rarely attribute that to its true source: his relationships, including those with his parents. The much more common reaction is to turn that inward and to conclude that he is not as worthwhile, or at least less worthwhile, than others. Once again this self-concept may operate outside of consciousness and be revealed in the boy's behavior and attitudes rather than in his conscious thinking.

Both Liam and Wesley exhibited self-hatred, though in different ways. Wesley abused alcohol and other drugs, failed to live up to his potential, and even attempted suicide—all clearly self-destructive behaviors that were driven by self-hatred. Liam's cutting was emblematic of his self-hatred. So was his self-imposed social isolation and his image of himself as unattractive.

There is no simple technique that will transform self-hatred into self-acceptance. Lest that statement cause you to feel hopeless, though, let me hasten to add that while there is no *simple* solution, it *is* possible for men with BPD to make this journey from self-hatred to self-acceptance. In fact, both Liam and Wesley did exactly that.

The key to finding self-acceptance lies partly within us and partly outside of us. What I mean by that is that the individual must be open to acceptance, but also must experience acceptance from others. Let me explain, using Wesley and Liam as examples.

WESLEY'S ROAD TO SELF-ACCEPTANCE

Wesley spent several days in the hospital. At first he was sullen and angry—and also detoxing from acute alcohol intoxication. On his third day he met Gabe, a man in his thirties, who introduced himself as a social worker on the hospital staff. Gabe spent several hours over the next couple of days talking to Wesley, who found himself gradually opening up to Gabe despite his initial hesitation. It was the most time Wesley had ever spent talking with another person in his life, and Gabe was the first person Wesley ever told about his abuse at the hands of his stepbrother. This was a major breakthrough for Wesley, who had always avoided talking about his past and who was ashamed of himself for being a victim of physical and sexual abuse. And because Wesley could not accept that about himself, he did not expect others to accept him. But Gabe surprised him.

Gabe not only accepted Wesley but sympathized with him. He told Wesley that he could understand his shame, as Gabe had talked with other men who'd been in the same position as Wesley—and every one of them, Gabe said, experienced that shame. It kept them from opening up and being able to confide in others. It left them isolated, Gabe said. Wesley could relate to that; he'd always felt like he was alone in the world, he told Gabe, even when he was with one of his many girlfriends. He could never allow himself to get close, he said.

Gabe's acceptance of Wesley had healing power. But that acceptance alone was not sufficient to heal Wesley. For that healing to begin, Wesley needed to be open to Gabe's acceptance. If he had rejected it, he would have gone on hating himself and being burdened by shame.

The second big step that Wesley took happened when Gabe asked if he could introduce a friend to Wesley, and Wesley agreed. Gabe set the stage for this by explaining that he would not disclose any of what Wesley had shared about his past abuse, but that he thought this friend might be of help to Wesley.

This second man, Nelson, turned out to be an addict who had been in recovery for five years. Wesley took an immediate liking to Nelson, but when Gabe suggested that Wesley think about going to a few twelve-step meetings with Nelson, Wesley stiffened and frowned. "I'm not saying that you're an addict," Gabe said. Nelson nodded in agreement. "However, I think you'd agree that you've already done more than your fair share of drinking and drugging, and it makes you depressed. We all know what happened that night when you were really drunk. I'm thinking that maybe you should stop drinking, at least for now.

Nelson is willing to go to a few meetings with you. If you don't like the program after that, fine. All I'm asking is that you give it a try and keep an open mind."

What Wesley did not share with Gabe or Nelson during that initial conversation was his expectation that the people at the twelve-step meetings would not like him. He believed they might see him as a "loser," or even suspect (correctly) that he'd been the victim of abuse. Also, the idea that he might possibly suffer from the disease of addiction (like his biological father) added to Wesley's self-image as "damaged goods." In other words, the last thing Wesley expected from a twelve-step meeting was acceptance. But that's exactly what he found.

Many people in recovery relate to the idea that while they were actively drinking and using other drugs, their self-image was very poor. Many relate to being burdened by shame. And many express shock at the acceptance and support they received through their recovery fellowships. That acceptance—call it unconditional love—is probably as vital to recovery as any advice offered in books or by therapists.

Wesley connected to the program of recovery and it, along with regular counseling sessions with Gabe, came to be his pathway to self-acceptance.

LIAM'S PATHWAY TO SELF-ACCEPTANCE

As was true for Wesley, Liam's path to self-acceptance began with a single relationship and a single event, and that was Anna's friendship. Just as Wesley took a first step toward healing himself when he opened himself to talking to Gabe, Liam took that first crucial step when he opened himself to those lunchtime conversations with Anna. And as Gabe had accepted Wesley, Anna had accepted Liam. Equally important, Liam allowed himself to open up to Anna's acceptance. That in turn challenged Liam's view of himself as unattractive and boring—in other words, second best.

Liam eventually took a risk and opened himself more to Anna, sharing with her the facts of his family life and the embarrassment he felt about his father. He did so with measurable trepidation, half-expecting to be rejected. But Anna did not reject him; on the contrary, she told Liam that she admired him for doing so well considering his family life. She also told him that she liked the fact that he was a sensitive person, as reflected in his drawings and poetry.

Liam's other big step was to see a therapist. There again, he found acceptance and sympathy. He was able to talk about his insecurity, especially his insecurity about his relationship with Anna. He opened up about his cutting and came to see how it had been his way of coping with free-floating anxiety. He gained some insight into the MBPD traits that were part of his personality, and came to realize that he could control or even eliminate them over time. At the time of our last meeting Liam and Anna were still dating (it had been over a year) and Anna had recently come out and told Liam that she loved him. He, of course, had wanted and hoped to hear those exact words.

Some Suggestions for Facilitating Self-Acceptance

In addition to finding their respective pathways to self-acceptance, Liam and Wesley benefited from practicing a few simple techniques on a regular basis. These are as follows.

TAKE A DEEP BREATH AND DON'T JUMP TO CONCLUSIONS

Men with Borderline Personality Disorder go through life being vigilant for rejection or abandonment. This was definitely true for Liam and Wesley, though their respective responses were somewhat different. Liam simply avoided social contact, as if he'd given up on relationships, concluding (unconsciously) that he was "second-best" and had little to offer. Wesley, in contrast, dealt with his insecurity by making unreasonable demands for attention from his girlfriends and then exploding when he didn't get it. He also tried to escape from his shame at being "damaged goods" through the use of alcohol and other drugs, and ultimately through attempting suicide.

Because they are on a hair trigger for signs of rejection, men with MBPD often jump to the conclusion that they are being rejected when in reality it isn't warranted. A BPD man may notice, for example, when his wife or partner smiles at someone at a party, but then conclude not that his partner is being social and friendly, but that this small interaction is an indication that his wife or partner is flirting or is interested in that someone. He may not even be consciously aware of having jumped to that conclusion, but it's revealed in his behavior: being angry, irritable, or depressed, or drinking too much.

At other times the man with MBPD may actually be aware of the false conclusion he's reached, yet he still reacts as if it were true. This happens often. As an example, a girlfriend may not return an email, text message, or phone message as promptly as the BPD man would like. He may try telling himself that she is probably just busy, yet he will become anxious or even angry. Or a spouse may express mild annoyance at something the BPD man does. On one level he may understand both the cause and the rationality of this reaction, yet he reacts as if he has concluded that his spouse does not love him and is rejecting him.

In addition to the mindfulness meditation technique described earlier, a simple technique that men like Liam and Wesley benefited from was to "take a deep breath and tell themselves to not jump to conclusions" whenever they were feeling upset or angry at their partner. I mean that literally. Taking that one deep breath can help a man settle down and rethink the situation. He can then ask himself one or more of the following questions:

- Am I really being rejected here? Is that what my partner is intending?

- Does my partner really believe I am "second-best" or "damaged goods," or am I reading that into this situation?

- Are my expectations for my partner's attention reasonable, or do I sometimes expect more than is humanly possible? Is that what is happening here?

OPEN YOURSELF TO ACCEPTANCE

Self-hatred is insidious. By its very nature it prevents one from taking the actions that are necessary to rid oneself of it. Self-hatred causes a man to close himself to the acceptance of others and its healing powers. Wesley could have elected not to open up to Gabe, assuming that Gabe would not like him, or would believe he was mentally ill, or that Wesley really was damaged goods. Wesley could have come up with any number of reasons to stay closed to Gabe's acceptance.

Similarly, he could have come up with many reasons not to go to those twelve-step meetings with Nelson. He could have said, "I'm not that bad-off." Or, he could have gone to one meeting and concluded he was "not like those people." Or he could simply have sat there and not communicated with others. But he chose a different course—one that opened the door to the possibility of healing and self-esteem. The factor that made the difference, he explained, was the acceptance that he experienced at the meetings he attended. "Every one of the people in those rooms were flawed," he said. "Yet they all respected—even loved—one another despite their flaws. I know that helped me see myself in a different light."

It takes a bit of courage or a leap of faith to open ourselves to acceptance, whether we have Borderline Personality Disorder or not. Men in our society are socialized to be strong and competitive. Revealing a weakness or a vulnerability runs contrary to the expectations that most men have for themselves. This is even more true, of course, for men with MBPD, who bear the additional burden of self-hatred.

ADD BALANCE TO YOUR LIFESTYLE

Both Liam and Wesley led what you might call "unbalanced" lifestyles. Despite his academic success, Liam was largely a social isolate. And though he'd had many girlfriends, Wesley did not have a single close male friend and he was adrift, with no goal in life. Both could benefit from moving their lives in the direction of greater balance, and they did so.

Liam learned though counseling that his social isolation, while "protecting" him from being rejected, also made him vulnerable to loneliness and free-floating anxiety. He could not expect Anna to be his total and complete social life, or the "cure" for his anxiety and insecurity. So with some coaching from his therapist Liam began visiting the college's fitness center three times a week, where he would spend about forty-five minutes using a stationary bike, a treadmill, and an elliptical trainer. The college also boasted an indoor swimming pool, and after a while Liam took to visiting it as well. In addition to getting him out of his room, this activity afforded the opportunity for some social interaction. This small change in routine marked the starting point for adding some "balance" to Liam's lifestyle.

Liam then started attending some of the free lectures, exhibits, and other public events offered by the college. He found, somewhat to his surprise, that people were friendly toward him and receptive on the few occasions when he offered a comment or opinion. He brought these experiences into his relationship with Anna, and found that they shared many of the same opinions, preferences, and even biases. In this way Liam's lifestyle became both richer and more balanced.

As for Wesley, getting involved in a recovery fellowship added depth and balance to his lifestyle. This is generally true, regardless of the twelve-step recovery fellowship a man chooses. Within six months Wesley had chosen a home group that he made sure to attend every week, along with two other meetings, at least one of which he'd also attend weekly. It was in a men's meeting that he found his first sponsor, a man in his fifties who'd been in recovery for twenty years and who took Wesley under his wing.

The sponsor-sponsee relationship is one that both requires and engenders trust. Because of the trust developed working the Twelve Steps with his sponsor, when that man brought up the issue of Wesley's lack of personal goals, Wesley didn't take offense. His sponsor asserted that Wesley was certainly smart enough to tackle the course work, and encouraged him to take one course a semester at a local community college. It didn't matter what courses Wesley chose, his sponsor said, adding that sooner or later Wesley would get an idea of a career that appealed to him. Or not; it didn't matter. But by following this advice, Wesley added yet more balance and depth to his life.

SUMMING UP

Self-hatred is a core element of Borderline Personality Disorder. It has its roots in experiences that lead a boy to conclude that he is either "second-best" as compared to others, or, perhaps worse, "damaged goods" that no one wants. Rarely is the boy who will grow to be the MBPD man consciously aware of his self-concept, yet it drives much of his behavior and attitudes.

The antidote for self-hatred comes through experiences of acceptance. But we must be open to such experiences in order to benefit from their healing power. Finally, men with MBPD often lead unbalanced life styles that only worsen their isolation and confirm their negative self-image. Creating more balance in their lifestyles can facilitate their recovery from Borderline Personality Disorder.

CHAPTER TEN

Boundaries: Me, You, and Us

At first Lisa had been flattered by all the attention that was being bestowed upon her by Ethan. She had dated him only a few times and he already was texting her several times a day, telling her that he was thinking about her and asking about how her day was going. She'd been a bit taken back when he wrote, "I can't stop thinking about you," but then dismissed it as something any man might say when he was pursuing a woman.

Lisa had recently broken off a two-year relationship with a man who, she'd finally concluded, had taken advantage of her while giving very little in return. The contrast between that man and Ethan made Ethan all the more appealing to her. After all, who wouldn't like all that attention? Who wouldn't like hearing that someone can't get you off their mind?

You, Me, and Us

One way to look at relationships is in terms of a Venn diagram, as pictured here:

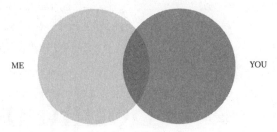

ME   YOU

In this diagram, one circle can be thought of as "me." The other circle represents "you" as my partner. As the diagram suggests, each person is to some degree a separate entity, an individual. The area of the diagram where the circles overlap can be thought of as "us," meaning that it depicts our relationship.

Relationships can vary significantly with respect to how large the shared us area is as compared to how large the individual, you and me areas are. For some couples a relatively limited us area is adequate. In contrast, consider what has been written about the relationship between John Lennon and Yoko Ono, which has been depicted (in words and pictures) as very intense and interconnected. This couple was often inseparable; consequently their relationship had a very large us area. Then there are couples whose individual careers, legislators who live in Washington and return home to their partners or families on weekends, for example, require them to spend large amounts of time apart. For these couples the us area may be important, but also much smaller than the me and you areas.

HOW MUCH US?

Just how large the shared us area should be is debatable and largely up to each couple to decide. That said, most people would agree that in order for a relationship to be "healthy," in the sense of balancing individuality with commonality, there needs to be some of both.

For many men with borderline personality, large areas of individuality in a relationship are threatening. They evoke free-floating anxiety and insecurity. What these men seek is maximum us and minimum you and me. That was true, Lisa learned, for Ethan.

It took about six months for Lisa to go from feeling flattered to beginning to feel smothered, and consequently ambivalent about her relationship with Ethan. On the one hand there was much she liked about him. She thought he was a good, kind person. They shared an interest in art and classic films that Lisa had discovered was rare in the men she'd dated. They liked the same food, and the same music. Finally, Ethan, like Lisa, preferred reading over watching television. Lisa also liked the fact that Ethan was a sensitive man (perhaps a bit too sensitive, she'd later conclude) who seemed to be able to read her feelings better than any man she'd dated. Altogether this made for some nice common ground on which to build a relationship.

On the other hand, Lisa found, Ethan was extremely thin-skinned. His feelings could be easily hurt. He could sink into a sullen mood quickly, and without any obvious provocation. After a while she realized it was most often in response to his feeling that she had somehow "blown him off." When she asked him if that was possible, Ethan nodded. Then he explained to Lisa how he would wait for her to respond to each and every text message he'd send to her. The longer he waited, the more anxious he would get. Then, if a few hours had passed, he'd get depressed. At times it distracted him from his work as an architect.

Lisa did believe it was important for two people in an intimate relationship to stay in touch with each other, and to share their thoughts and feelings. In that way she did not mind, and even appreciated, Ethan's text messages. However, she was uncomfortable with the idea that she was obligated to respond—and quickly—to each and every one of Ethan's messages. Still, she decided that it would not be too difficult for her to respond to a message from Ethan within an hour; that is, if she was not too busy at work, and as long as there were no more than two or three a day. Ethan agreed that that made sense. So Lisa tried that and it seemed to ease Ethan's anxiety—for a while.

As Ethan's borderline personality emerged more strongly, Lisa discovered that what he wanted, in her words, "Was not a relationship, but a complete loss of individuality." What she meant was that Ethan was uncomfortable with virtually any separate me and you, and instead wanted the relationship to be pretty much all us. This was revealed not so much in his words as in his actions. After a while, it became apparent that he wanted to know where Lisa was, all the time. He became obviously uncomfortable when she told him she was meeting with a couple of girlfriends. And if she was as little as ten minutes late meeting him he'd ask, in a tone that communicated suspicion, where she'd been. If she replied that traffic had slowed her down he'd nod, but look distinctly unhappy. And so on. Those, of course, were all signs of Ethan's MBPD, and they spelled trouble for that relationship.

Celebrating Differences

People with borderline traits are often driven to maximize the us in a relationship, and some people would go so far as to argue that those with severe MBPD are driven to virtually eliminate the you, leaving only me and us remaining. That may be true, but let's focus here on men whose MBPD is more moderate. For these men, the idea of differences may not be intolerable, but it does evoke anxiety. Why? One likely reason is that, from the perspective of the man with MBPD, differences may be misinterpreted as rejection or abandonment. That's right: rejection or abandonment. But, you might ask, how can that be? Why should the fact, for example, that a MBPD man prefers spending free time engaged in solitary activities, while his partner enjoys social activities, make that man anxious? How could he perceive it as rejection or abandonment?

To understand the above we need to keep in mind that the insecurity that lies at the core of the borderline personality and temperament has roots that run deep in his past. As a youth this man experienced frequent interactions that communicated ambivalence toward him or outright rejection. Rather than seeing this as a problem within those he expected to love and protect him, the boy blamed himself for being either second-best or damaged goods. Very often it was some perceived difference or differences between himself and someone else that he saw as the reason for his being rejected or abandoned. He may reach these conclusions consciously, but more likely they operated on an unconscious level. In other words, the boy did not step back, assess his situation accurately, and realize that there was nothing wrong with him. Instead, he saw himself as flawed, thus stoking his self-hatred.

In this scheme, you can see how a boy could conclude (again, unconsciously) that acceptance and security lie in sameness, whereas differences represent treacherous territory in relationships. You can be rejected for being different. A boy may even go so far as to identify with a rejecting or ambivalent parent, and go on as an adult to replicate this pattern in his own relationships.

There is only one way to break out of this pattern, and in turn to break free from insecurity and free-floating anxiety, and that is to learn not only to tolerate but to celebrate differences. As a man with MBPD is able to move from intolerance to tolerance, and from tolerance to celebration, he opens the door to truly fulfilling relationships.

IDENTIFYING SIMILARITIES AND DIFFERENCES

The key here is for a man with BPD traits to be open to identifying and then accepting significant differences between himself and his partner. Such differences can include interests, but they can also include traits and temperaments. It's the latter, much more than differences in interests, that tend to make the man with BPD uncomfortable.

As a first step, go through the following list of traits and temperaments. For each one, identify first where you fall, using a **Y**. Next, identify where your partner's personality falls on each of these dimensions, using a **P**. You can copy this diagram onto a separate piece of paper so that you can refer to it at a later date.

Personality Profile

Outgoing _____ Shy

Assertive (Outspoken) _____ Unassertive (Reserved)

Adventurous _____ Cautious

Competitive _____ Cooperative

Inclined to Spend _____ Inclined to Save

Optimistic _____ Pessimistic

Happy-go-lucky _____ Somber

Organized _____ Disorganized

Spontaneous _____ Deliberate

Confident _____ Unconfident

Dreamer _____ Planner

Feel free to add more personality/temperament dimensions if they occur to you. Again, place yourself and your partner where you believe each of you fits on any dimensions you create.

The second step in this exercise is to identify those dimensions on which there is the greatest difference, in your opinion, between you and your partner. Finding ways to accommodate such differences can be challenging in any relationship. Some say that opposites attract, and this may be true. It strikes me from my work with couples that we can be attracted to someone who possesses traits we wish we had more of. For example, the shy man may be drawn to an outgoing partner. Someone who feels that his or her life is too disorganized, or who has trouble managing money, may be drawn to the opposite: someone who is organized and frugal. The cautious individual may be drawn to an adventurous one. And so on. For these people their relationship then becomes complementary.

Complementary relationships certainly can work. The challenge they face, however, is for the couple to accept and respect those differences, recognizing in a sense that they are stronger and more adaptable as a couple than either partner would be as an individual. If an adventurous person who can't manage money were to match up with a cautious and frugal partner, for example, they both could conceivably enjoy the benefits of a life of travel and discovery, but without going broke.

The problem for some couples is that, over time, the very qualities that attracted them to one another have a way of becoming annoyances, or even areas of conflict. Men with significant borderline traits often fall victim to this tendency to eventually dislike or even resent the very qualities they are initially attracted to in a partner. But sustaining a successful complementary relationship requires the capacity to recognize and embrace significant amounts of individuality (me and you) along with an area of commonality (us). It is those very differences that lead partners to have different interests, and to interact with others in different ways. But because those very differences can be interpreted (unconsciously) by the borderline man as sign of rejection or ambivalence, he will become anxious about them and want to eliminate them so as to feel more secure.

EMBRACING DIFFERENCES

So, you now have faced up to the reality that you and your loved one have personalities and temperaments that include at least a few significant differences. The questions you must face now are these:

- How comfortable, versus uncomfortable, are you with these differences?

- Which differences in particular make you most uncomfortable?

- Could any of these differences present a threat to your relationship? If so, which one(s), and how could they be a threat?

- Do you think that, on some level, you may at times have interpreted differences between you as meaning your partner was ambivalent about your relationship, or even rejecting of you?

- If you answered yes to the last question, think of a few examples of times when this happened.

- Can you imagine how the differences between you and your partner could make you stronger and more resilient as a couple?

Giving some thought to the above questions can start you down the path from rejecting differences and being threatened by them, to accepting and even embracing them. In time you may come to appreciate how these differences make you more adaptable and resilient as a couple than either of you might be as individuals.

Even better than simply giving it some thought is to engage in a dialogue, either with your partner or with a therapist, about differences and how they can be misunderstood. It's important to recognize our own personalities and temperaments, and how they can represent strengths as well as vulnerabilities. As an example of temperament, consider those who might describe themselves as "thrifty" or "frugal." The qualities associated with thrift and frugality will probably color other areas of their lives. Cautious and guarded about money, they may find themselves leading a cautious, guarded life. They will live a safe, though perhaps limited, lifestyle without much adventure or spontaneity. No problem. But in a relationship with one whose basic temperamental values are adventure and spontaneity, this difference could create misunderstandings and frustrations.

If he works at it, a man with MBPD can gradually come to be less bothered by differences between himself and his loved one and less inclined to want to make those differences disappear. Eventually he may even come to value them.

TOLERATING SEPARATION

You've heard the phrase, "joined at the hip." It's a phrase that can be used good-naturedly to describe a high degree of closeness between friends, or in a more negative way, to describe an annoyingly clingy couple who can always be counted on to act in unison. So much depends on the persons doing the describing as well as those being so described.

Being joined at the hip implies a lack of separation or individuality. For some couples this may have some appeal. It may be appealing, for example, to couples who both have borderline traits and who seek comfort in melding from two individuals (me and you) into one (us). I have known couples like that from time to time and they've seemed quite happy; although they also tended to be insular, having few close friends and spending virtually all of their time together.

For the majority of people, though, some degree of individuality and separation represents a healthy balance to their relationships. They prefer, in other words, at least a bit of me in addition to more of us. That's how it was for Lisa in her relationship with Ethan. He, however, seemed to want something different. The result? From Ethan's perspective he was simply seeking closeness; but from Lisa's perspective it felt like she was being smothered.

Since she'd been a young girl Lisa had always possessed an independent spirit. In relationships she described herself as someone who was not a "player," and who had never "cheated" on a boyfriend. In that regard, she was certain Ethan had nothing to worry about if she decided they should become partners. Like him, her long-term goal was marriage and a family. At the same time she was committed to her passion of long-distance running, as well as to her relationships with a small circle of close women friends. A couple of these were fellow runners and every fall they would enter several five- or ten-mile runs that were held in various New England towns. A few she would meet occasionally for coffee or an early dinner after work. And once a year the whole group got together for a long weekend at the Rhode Island shore.

Lisa was willing to respond to Ethan's text messages in a timely manner; but she was not willing to give up this other part of her life. That meant that she and Ethan might be spending significant time together, but not virtually all of their time together. And that spelled trouble for this otherwise promising relationship.

Fortunately for Ethan, he was self-aware enough (and wanted this relationship enough) to own up to his anxiety and talk to Lisa about it. He knew that on some level his anxiety was unreasonable, even irrational. Objectively, he did trust Lisa. Also objectively, he recognized that her friendships were as much a part of who Lisa was as were her interests and her work as an information technology specialist. Yet despite this objective knowledge Ethan could not seem to get past his discomfort whenever Lisa was away from him (and with others), or when he found himself waiting for a return text message, or waiting for her to show up at his place for dinner.

Ethan's anxiety, as has been true for the other men described here, was operating on an unconscious level. It was a manifestation of his insecurity. I will not describe his background in detail but suffice it to say that his experiences as a boy were not unlike those of others who grow up to be men with BPD. In effect, separations from Lisa felt like abandonment to Ethan. And the more deeply he fell in love with Lisa, the more intense his insecurity became.

Ethan's solution (and the best hope for his relationship with Lisa) began when he was able to "connect the dots" and see the connection between parents who had shown definite ambivalence toward him and his deep insecurity. He had been the only child of two professionals, neither of whom had apparently ever been wholly comfortable with parenthood. As Ethan put it, "I had every advantage, materially, growing up; but my upbringing was also 'outsourced' to a series of nannies. Both of my parents could be attentive at times, and then just as easily turn their backs as they pursued very successful careers. I tried to please them—to get their attention—but in many ways I got the feeling that I was more or less a pain in the ass. Looking back I think they were basically happy together, but partly because they let each other devote a huge amount of time to their respective careers."

Armed with his insight, and working together with Lisa and the therapist, Ethan worked on addressing his anxiety when being separated from Lisa. Here are a few of the techniques that worked for him:

- *Distraction.* Ethan also had plenty of interests in his life. He even had a small circle of male friends. He practiced planning to distract himself when he knew Lisa would be with friends, either by pursuing one of his interests or arranging to meet with a friend for dinner. Ethan found that his friends liked that, and that the distraction helped. Prior to that what he'd do was to sit at home and ruminate about where Lisa was and what she was doing.

- *Imagining.* Rather than simply worrying that Lisa had lost interest in him (or worse, had found someone else), Ethan practiced imagining what Lisa was actually doing when he'd start to feel anxious. For example, he would imagine her busy at her desk at work—too busy to be able to return a text message. Or he'd picture her running in a road race alongside two of her women friends.

- *Label it and challenge it!* Earlier we saw that it helps to exorcise the demon of insecurity when you name and challenge it. That's exactly what Ethan learned to do. As soon as he'd begin feeling uncomfortable when he and Lisa were not together, or when he'd feel uncomfortable because she was late or had not returned his message, Ethan would label that feeling as free-floating anxiety and a manifestation of his insecurity. He then told himself the following:

  - I am not a child. My insecurity comes from my childhood but I am not a helpless child now.

• Lisa is not ambivalent about me.

• I am not being abandoned.

The above formed the basis for Ethan's recovery from the burdens of Borderline Personality Disorder. And as that got under control it looked like the future was bright for him and Lisa.

SUMMING UP

Establishing healthy boundaries and creating a relationship that balances individuality with togetherness can be a major challenge for the man with Borderline Personality Disorder. However, unless he establishes healthy boundaries, his loved ones will eventually feel smothered and resentful. It is entirely possible for a BPD man to create a self-fulfilling prophecy: resisting individuality, being distrustful, and demanding constant attention and reassurance to such a degree that he ends up driving away the very person he loves. By working on maintaining healthy boundaries and confronting their insecurity head-on these men can increase their chances of finding fulfilling relationships.

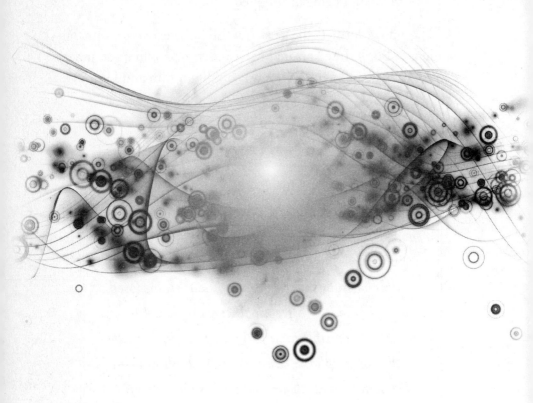

CHAPTER ELEVEN

Building Psychological Resilience

A central theme of this book has been that the problems of living associated with having Borderline Personality Disorder have largely been overlooked when it comes to men. As a result men with BPD, whether severe or moderate, are frequently misdiagnosed and mistreated. This was the case for Sean. Although the particulars of his story were unique to him, you as a reader will recognize the themes that by now should be familiar to you, and which are associated with MBPD.

Sean

It was actually Sean's wife, Maggie, who came to see me first. She said she was concerned because Sean, who had recently turned fifty, had also started to drink more. He'd always been a drinker, she explained—a one- or two-beer a night drinker—throughout their eighteen-year marriage. Maggie had once been married to a severe alcoholic whom she'd divorced after three years because he'd been totally unreliable and, eventually, abusive. So she was understandably sensitive to Sean's increased drinking.

Over the past six months, Maggie explained, as Sean's drinking had increased, Maggie thought he'd also become increasingly irritable and, from her perspective, depressed. That worried her, as Sean's irritability revived memories of Maggie's earlier abuse.

Sean and their only child, a fourteen-year-old daughter named Rachel, had a history of intermittent conflict that seemed to escalate the older Rachel got and the more she began to "feel her oats" and seek more independence. For example, recently Rachel and Maggie had argued over what kinds of clothing were appropriate to wear to school. Sean overheard them arguing, but instead of staying out of what was actually a fairly typical mother-daughter tussle, he'd butted in, only to end up yelling at Rachel. Also, Rachel had taken to spending more weekend nights sleeping over at one or another of her many girlfriends' homes. Sean had made a few comments about that as well, insinuating that Rachel thought her own home wasn't "good enough."

Sean and Rachel had had some pleasant moments, Maggie explained. But Sean had never been particularly affectionate toward his daughter. They rarely hugged. "I've never heard him say, 'I love you' to Rachel," Maggie said, "even though she still says that to him. I believe he does love her; he just can't seem to get the words out. She loves him too, though I can understand why she can be snippy with him at times."

Maggie described Sean as a hardworking and responsible husband who made a decent living as a self-taught carpenter, painter, and general handyman. Over the years he'd built up a substantial customer base as a result of the quality of his work and his ability to accommodate his customers' sometimes finicky needs.

About a year earlier Sean had injured his back. After a thorough medical assessment he was told that although surgery was not recommended, his condition could place some limits on what work he could do. Specifically, he'd had to hire an assistant to paint ceilings, so as to stay off high ladders; and he had to be careful about lifting anything heavy without assistance.

Though he still got up and went to work every day—even when he felt sick—Sean had begun expressing negative feelings about both his work and himself. "I've heard him say he's a failure," Maggie told me. I asked her why Sean might believe that. "He says he's fifty years old and has nothing to show for it. That's not really true, because we have a nice house and a delightful daughter. But I make as much money as he does, so maybe that's one reason he feels bad. He also said that he thinks his health is beginning to fail and he doesn't know how long he will be able to keep working as hard as he does."

I asked Maggie to tell me something about her marriage to Sean. "He's a good husband," she said. "He's always tried to be helpful around the house. He even helps with the cleaning. He likes to cook. But he's also always been a very jealous man. That probably has something to do with the fact that his first wife cheated on him and then kicked him out when he found out about it."

According to Maggie, Sean also had a strong sex drive. "He could have sex every night. I'm not always up for that. My sex drive has never been that strong. And I'm especially not up for sex when I'm upset or angry at him, like when he drinks too much and gets irritable. If I say I'm not interested, he'll sulk. There was a time when I'd give in to that just to make him happy, but I don't anymore."

I told Maggie that it sounded like Sean was experiencing some depression in addition to drinking more—and that the two could well be related. I suggested she ask him to come in to meet with me and was a bit surprised the next morning to discover that he'd called and left a message on my answering machine.

So Sean and I met. We spoke for an hour and a half on that first visit. Here is what I learned about Sean's past:

- He was the oldest of three sons. His father, a successful business man, had abandoned the family when Sean was ten and moved in with another woman who later became his wife and Sean's stepmother.

- Despite his financial success, Sean's father had paid very little in the way of support to Sean's mother as he had managed to get a very favorable divorce agreement. As a result, Sean's mother then had to get a full time job that also required a long commute. Household conditions for Sean and his brothers were financially tight.

- When Sean turned twelve his mother told him she could no longer afford to raise three children and that he would have to move in with his father. Sean did that, and lived with his father for six months. Every weekend Sean's stepmother would hand him fifty dollars and then tell him to "get lost." He'd spend those weekends with friends.

- After six months Sean moved in with a girlfriend and her mother. His stepmother agreed to keep giving him the weekly fifty dollars, which he handed over to the girlfriend's mother.

- Sean and his girlfriend married when they were both eighteen. Sean had sought out work from a local handyman, who taught Sean much of what he knew about carpentry. Sean became that man's apprentice of sorts, and he earned enough money to pay for an apartment for him and his girlfriend.

• About eighteen months into the marriage a friend told Sean that the word on the street was that his wife was cheating on him. When Sean confronted his wife, she refused to answer. A week later, however, she told him that she no longer loved him and wanted him to move out. She had a new "friend," she said, who could take over paying the rent. Sean left.

A familiar pattern? Indeed. Sean's upbringing had been one long story of rejection, ambivalence, and outright abandonment. It was an upbringing that was ripe for fostering a borderline personality, which is exactly what happened to Sean. Was he an unlovable man (or father)? No. But was he a man who could be "hard to love"? Definitely!

As an adult Sean manifested virtually all of the symptoms associated with MBPD. In particular he was insecure, and his comments about himself were a testament to how much he suffered from self-hatred. He sought comfort through sex, and was irrationally jealous. And he suffered from free-floating anxiety—a vague sense of dread about the future. I also thought there was a good chance that his daughter Rachel's increasing independence might be stirring up some unconscious feelings of abandonment in Sean, and that her conflict with him might feel like rejection to him. Maggie nodded, then she said that Sean often expressed feelings of being unappreciated, especially by Rachel. I also thought there was a good chance that Maggie's refusing sex could have felt like abandonment to Sean, rather than a simple difference in their sex drives (or her understandable reluctance when she was annoyed with him).

Resilience

One thing that many borderline men do—and this was very definitely the case with Sean—is to turn even relatively minor disappointments and frustrations into catastrophes. For as long as she'd known him, and in spite of how responsible he was, Sean had a capacity, in his wife's words, "to make mountains out of molehills." In other words, Sean could turn a minor mishap into a major catastrophe at the drop of a hat. Many MBPD men have this trait, just as they can perceive the slightest inattention as rejection or abandonment.

The tendency to "catastrophize" is a central part of what psychologists call a fragile personality. Over the past twenty years psychologists have learned about people who are able to weather life crises and emerge pretty much unscathed, versus those who don't. They use the word resilient to describe the former group, in contrast to those whose personalities could be described as fragile. The kinds of experiences that mark the formative years of men with MBPD predispose them to become psychologically fragile as adults.

HOW PSYCHOLOGICALLY RESILIENT ARE YOU?

You can use the following inventory to get a sense of just how resilient you are. Answer each question as it applies to you. After you answer each question, you can total your score to come up with a resilience index, which can range from zero to forty-five.

Resilience Inventory

Instructions: Respond to each of the following questions in terms of how well it describes you, from 0 (*not at all*) to 5 (*entirely*). When you are finished, total your scores.

1. I believe that I was put here for a purpose.

| 0 | 1 | 2 | 3 | 4 | 5 |

2. I believe in the saying, "For every door that closes, another door opens."

| 0 | 1 | 2 | 3 | 4 | 5 |

3. I believe my life has meaning.

| 0 | 1 | 2 | 3 | 4 | 5 |

4. I believe it's true that every cloud has a silver lining.

| 0 | 1 | 2 | 3 | 4 | 5 |

5. I believe every life crisis also presents us with opportunities.

| 0 | 1 | 2 | 3 | 4 | 5 |

6. I am someone who is willing to take risks.

| 0 | 1 | 2 | 3 | 4 | 5 |

7. I have always believed that I am the master of my own fate.

| 0 | 1 | 2 | 3 | 4 | 5 |

8. Being happy in life is up to me.

| 0 | 1 | 2 | 3 | 4 | 5 |

9. I am an optimist.

| 0 | 1 | 2 | 3 | 4 | 5 |

Total Score: _____ = Resilience Index

Take a look at your resilience index. Higher scores are associated with greater psychological resilience. How accurately do you think your responses describe you in terms of your true beliefs? Do you think you may have slanted your answers in one direction or another? In which direction does your personality lean: toward resilience or toward fragility?

Most people, if they take some time to reflect and answer the above questions honestly, find that their resilience index falls somewhere in the middle range. There are, of course, exceptions; that is, people who are unusually resilient. These people are optimists. They believe that occasional crises are a normal part of life. They expect them and when faced with a crisis they marshal their resources and spring into action. They also believe that every crisis presents an opportunity, if you are open to seeing it, and that difficulties can be overcome through persistence.

Conversely, there are people who fall at the opposite extreme. They are psychologically fragile. These are people who will have the hardest time getting through a crisis, and who are most likely to catastrophize. They are pessimistic and inclined to expect the worst, not the best. As opposed to believing that crises are a normal, expected part of life, they may feel that they are victims. Faced with a crisis they tend to feel helpless, more ready to give up than persist. In relationships, they are eternally vigilant for being rejected or abandoned.

Methods of Building Psychological Resilience

What should you do if you discover that your own resilience index appears to fall somewhere on the low end of the resilience index? Does this mean that you are in for hard times forever? The answer depends on whether or not you want to do something about it.

If you feel helpless to change your outlook on life, then the coming months (and possibly years) may indeed be painful and highly stressful for you. They may take a toll on your emotional and physical health as well as on your relationships.

On the other hand, if you choose to do so, it is possible to work on changing the way you approach life in general, including your relationships, so as to become more resilient. What follows are two tried-and-true methods that psychologists have used to help people move from a fragile to a resilient stance toward life.

SELF-TALK

Self-talk is straightforward. It means that you must make a habit of making resilient statements to yourself—statements like those that appear in the resilience inventory. There are many ways that you can prompt yourself to challenge your "non-resilient" thinking. For example, you can purchase a weekly calendar and write one resilient statement at the top of each week. Then each day when you open the calendar, read that week's resilient statement to yourself. You can also type out or write all nine resilient beliefs and then tape them up, individually or as a group, in a place where you will see them every day. For example, some people tack their list of resilient statements on a bulletin board in their office or work station. They then begin each day by taking a moment to read one or all of the beliefs. They then take another minute or so to pause, reflect, and give that belief a chance to sink in.

It may strike you as hard to believe, but self-talk has actually been found to be an effective method for changing thought patterns. The secret lies in the fact that most people are not consciously aware of their inner beliefs and how these beliefs affect them, much less where these beliefs come from. Of course, the formative years of those with MBPD tend to promote a psychologically fragile, as opposed to a resilient, outlook on life. Even resilient people, though, more or less just act in resilient ways, without being aware of the underlying beliefs that motivate their behavior. Similarly, the psychologically fragile person may not be consciously aware that a tendency toward fragility, for example, to be pessimistic and get easily discouraged, is actually based on an inner belief that he cannot effectively control his life, that his life has no meaning and purpose, and that he is destined to be abandoned. It's easy to see how these different approaches to life will lead to very different outcomes; in fact, they often turn a life into a self-fulfilling prophecy. So, if you use this self-talk technique conscientiously for a period of time, you can expect your behavior (and the quality of your life) to change.

COGNITIVE ROLE-PLAYING

A second effective method for changing beliefs (and, in turn, behavior) is called "cognitive role-playing." This is just a fancy term for what boils down to imagining yourself in different situations and then imagining how you would react in each situation depending on what beliefs you held. Here is an example:

> Your spouse was scheduled today for an MRI of the spine to help determine if a disk problem is the cause of fairly intense lower back pain that started about a month ago. You have two children, ages six and eight. Your family enjoys a comfortable lifestyle, but that lifestyle is dependent on both you and your spouse working full-time. You have just left your job for the day and are on your way to pick up the children from their after-school day care facility—a responsibility you and your spouse alternate. Your cell phone rings. You answer. It's your spouse, sounding decidedly upset. He (she) blurts out the news: "They found a small tumor. The doctor believes it is probably benign, but that's what's causing the pain. But she wants me to go for a biopsy tomorrow."

There are two ways to respond to the above hypothetical situation, and these will depend in part on how psychologically resilient versus fragile you are. Naturally, it is appropriate to be alarmed at hearing this news. Beyond that, your initial reaction will also depend on what you believe about life and life crises. Imagine yourself being in the above situation, and then imagine how you would react if you held one or both of the following psychologically fragile beliefs:

- The tumor is malignant. My family and my life will fall apart.

- I'm cursed—doomed to suffer.

If you imagine having such beliefs in this kind of situation, chances are you feel scared and powerless, and perhaps hopeless. You may experience an urge to run and hide somewhere.

Now, imagine being in this same situation, but this time try on the following beliefs for size and see how you react:

- This is serious, but even if the tumor is malignant there may be treatments.

- Whatever happens, I will be there to make sure my children are okay; and we will find a way to come out of this just fine.

How do you feel when you view this situation through the "lens" of the above resilient beliefs? Do you still feel as anxious? Does the situation seem hopeless? Do you feel like running away, or standing your ground?

Cognitive role-playing, like self-talk, really can work. It gives you a chance to try on a "new set of glasses," psychologically speaking, and to see how the world looks through these new lenses. The example given of a tumor can easily be translated into an example involving an issue in your relationship.

Your wife tells you over dinner that she would like to accept her friends' invitation to join them on a long weekend outing to Las Vegas. You know she had done such activities before she met you, and even after you'd met, but before you were married, she continued to take part. You know her friends. They are now also married. For years this tight circle

*of friends had had a tradition of such a yearly get-together in
some curious place. Now they want to renew that tradition.*

Imagine how you would react if you were to hear the above
request but had a psychologically fragile outlook as exemplified
by the following beliefs:

- I am not lovable or valuable enough for my wife.
- I'm sure my wife will be flirting with other men on this trip.
- This is a serious threat to my marriage.

You would almost certainly feel very anxious if you were to
view your wife's request through the above "lens." If she were to
go on this adventure with her friends you would feel pessimistic
about your marriage but helpless to do anything about it. You
might get either very depressed or angry. In either case you
might put up a strong resistance, which in turn could actually
hurt your relationship.

Now, imagine hearing this same request, only this time
through the following psychologically resilient lens:

- My marriage is secure and my wife loves me.
- I will miss her, but spending time with her close friends on a
  yearly excursion is good for my wife and our marriage.
- I will have no trouble finding something to do that weekend.

Surely you can feel the difference. Yes, you will miss your
wife; at the same time you see this trip as important to your wife's
overall well-being, and something that will only strengthen
your marriage.

This example may present a scenario that strikes you as a bit
extreme, but for the man with a borderline personality, something
as minor as his partner stopping to meet a friend for a cup of

coffee after work (or stopping at a fitness club to exercise) can evoke insecurity and anxiety—and so he may resist it. In doing so, however, he could be damaging his relationship.

Imagine a situation or circumstance in your relationship that could make you anxious. Then, see how you feel when you look at that situation through a psychologically resilient set of lenses. Practice this daily, and in time you will find that you react differently in your day-to-day interactions. Equally important, your relationship will improve.

SEAN'S SOLUTION

Sean actually made use of many of the suggestions that have been presented here in Part Two of the book. But the first step he took was to "connect the dots" and see how his adult traits and behaviors were rooted in insecurity that had its origins in his formative years. That was not an easy thing for Sean to do. He had not thought much about his childhood for many years, and he was not eager to begin doing so now. At first he was even reluctant to state that he'd experienced rejection and abandonment as a child, and that he had in fact been treated as if he were second-best.

Eventually Sean came to accept, however, that rejection and abandonment had been his reality, and that that reality had a direct connection to the borderline traits he'd developed as an adult man. These included his insecurity and self-hatred, his need for reassurance through sex, and even the anxiety that was generated by his daughter's growing independence. Absent that insight, Sean would be left to try to make sense of his unhappiness, his anxiety, and how he'd managed both in part through drinking, without any context for understanding his emotions and his behavior.

When Sean first began to make the connection between his past and his adult personality he experienced periodic bouts of sadness. Significantly, he did not feel self-hatred or free-floating anxiety. Rather, what he felt was akin to grief. He did not feel angry at his mother, who he knew had only been trying to do her best under extreme circumstances. He knew she loved him, despite the fact that she'd made him leave and live with his father.

Sean's feelings toward his father were another matter altogether. He had not seen or spoken to the man for many years, and he had no desire to as he came to realize the damage that his father's abandonment had done, not only to him but to his brothers as well. Most of all he resented the fact that his father could easily have afforded to support him and his brothers financially, but had been too selfish to do so. When he thought about his father now, Sean felt angry—justifiably, in my opinion. But he decided not to pursue it, believing there would be nothing to gain other than venting his rage.

At the same time, Sean reported feeling somewhat better about himself. He'd known for a long time that he was hard on himself, inclined toward self-hatred. But as he put his upbringing into perspective, Sean found that such feelings were beginning to dissipate. I explained to him that this was probably because, as a boy, he blamed himself for his father leaving, as well as for his mother farming him out. From his perspective as a child he could only feel that he was somehow second-best. But as he came to see how it had not been him, but his father and mother who were responsible for what happened, Sean was able to begin the process of self-acceptance.

Sean also availed himself, over a period of a year, of many of the other solutions that were presented in earlier chapters, beginning with meditation. This too was something foreign to him, and I could tell from his initial reaction that perhaps I was suggesting something he saw as mystical or cult-like. But to his credit Sean was willing to give it a try and after a few weeks he reported that he actually looked forward to meditating for about fifteen minutes when he got home from work every day. An added benefit was that by making that change in his daily routine Sean was able to put off having that first beer. Within a couple of months his drinking had decreased significantly. He still enjoyed a beer, but by then it was usually only one, with dinner.

Another part of Sean's solution was to add some balance to his lifestyle. A hard worker and a good provider, Sean had never been very generous with himself. His wife was used to buying his clothes, for example, and when she would ask what he wanted for his birthday Sean typically shrugged, as he hadn't given it any thought.

When I suggested that Sean look into a family membership at a local fitness center his first response was that it would probably be too expensive. I replied that it was my impression that membership fees for such places had decreased significantly in recent years. I explained that most also had personal trainers who could help design a program of exercise that might even strengthen Sean's back over time.

When Sean brought up the idea at home both Maggie and Rachel jumped at it. Rachel was, of course, as preoccupied with her physical appearance as any teen. The idea of regular exercise and how it could tone her up was very appealing. She'd never liked exercising at home; besides, she had several friends who made use of the fitness center her father had mentioned. And as if to add icing to the cake, it also boasted a lap pool!

Maggie, unlike Rachel, had been exercising regularly at home for years. She'd wake up half an hour before everyone else and hit a treadmill that was in their finished basement. She'd suggested to Sean on several occasions that he give it a try but he'd never seemed interested. Though she would never have brought it up herself, she liked the idea of the fitness center immediately, not only because she thought it would be good for Sean, but because it represented the first activity that they could engage in as a family—something that Maggie had long thought was sorely missing from their family life.

Indeed, the fitness center did form a focus for this family. Sean and Maggie would go there once or twice during the week, and again once on weekends. Rachel occasionally went with them, but she also would hitch rides with friends. When there she did not spend a whole lot of time with her parents; on the other hand, they would often run into one another. Also, she would occasionally join them for a smoothie at the club's health bar after their workouts. Finally, she would sometimes have brief conversations at home with either Sean or Maggie about what she and they were doing at the club. That may seem like a minor change, but it represented a major leap in Sean's relationship with his daughter.

As all of the above was slowly taking place, Sean was also working on finding his voice. More hard work! Because he'd never identified the source of his unhappiness and self-hatred, he really had never labeled it, much less expressed it. This too was difficult for a man who, if he took pride in nothing else, took pride in his ruggedness. In addition, Sean had so many years of experience either ignoring or suppressing his feelings that he didn't recognize either anxiety or insecurity for what they really were. And when he finally did recognize and identify those feelings he didn't expect them to be acceptable to others.

Sean worked together with Maggie on this. He also role-played expressing his feelings in therapy sessions. He practiced identifying insecurity and free-floating anxiety, labeling them, and then saying out loud how he was feeling. We talked about how such feelings embarrassed him, and how he expected others (especially Maggie, but also to some extent me as another man) to react.

As so often happens, as Sean worked on finding his voice (and experienced acceptance from Maggie) his insecurity and anxiety gradually diminished. As was said earlier, insecurity often lingers, and it did so for Sean. But after a while it was no longer disabling.

Last but not least, Sean utilized the cognitive techniques described earlier in this chapter in an effort to move his overall outlook on life from one that was psychologically fragile toward one that was more psychologically resilient. He readily admitted that he'd always been a pessimist—always expecting the worst. Again, he hadn't really given it much thought, but he found that if he imagined various scenarios and then viewed them from a psychologically resilient perspective his reactions were very different from what he was accustomed to.

As an example, we imagined a time when Sean's daughter Rachel would announce that she had her first boyfriend. Given Rachel's age and the fact that she was a bright and attractive teen, that event was probably not far off. As I suspected, if Sean imagined this event through his pessimistic, psychologically fragile "lens" of pessimism he might have felt upset and even a bit depressed. As we talked it out he realized that what he expected was that his daughter would one day "abandon" him for some man in her life, or that father and daughter might even become alienated. Sean understood very well that Rachel would one day move into the next developmental stage of her life. He even knew that was healthy. At the same time, his insecurity could also be set off by that event.

Then Sean imagined this same event through a psychologically resilient "lens": Rachel was someone who had much to offer in life, she was a loving child, and she also loved both her mother and father. The bond between Sean and Rachel could never be broken—it would merely change as Rachel matured.

Viewed from the latter perspective, the prospect of his daughter moving on to the dating stage of her life was much less anxiety-provoking for Sean. He could practice telling himself that the bond between him and Rachel was, if anything, getting stronger as his own lifestyle and outlook changed, and as the family grew closer through shared activities.

SUMMING UP

The "lens" through which we view the world, and our expectations for our lives, exerts a profound influence on our behavior. Experiences that involve parental ambivalence, abandonment, or rejection set a boy up to develop a psychologically fragile stance toward life that can be very disabling. In this chapter we explored ways to assess your own psychological resilience and to try out ways to move from fragility toward resilience. We also saw how one man was able to make use of a number of the solutions presented here to gradually break free from his borderline personality traits.

CHAPTER TWELVE

Fathering: Opportunity for a Fresh Start

At the same time that they worked to free themselves of the borderline traits that stood between themselves and a fulfilling lifestyle, many of the men described in this book found themselves confronted with a parallel challenge: to not repeat the very patterns that created their issues with their own children. Sean, whose story was told earlier, is a typical example.

Although he loved his daughter Rachel dearly, in some respects Sean had already related to her in ways that were detrimental to her self-esteem and overall mental health. Because of his own insecurity Sean had related to Rachel in ways that would very likely come across to her as reflecting ambivalence toward her on his part. That in turn could recreate the very insecurity in Rachel that Sean had struggled with all his life.

Fortunately, Rachel was not exposed to anything close to the kinds of rejection and abandonment that her father had known during his formative years. She did know that her father loved her, despite what she thought of as his "moodiness." He was a steady provider, and always generous with his daughter. Rachel also had a good relationship with her mother. So, all considered, Rachel was a much more psychologically resilient individual, even as a teenager, than her father had ever been. Still, Rachel stood to benefit if her relationship with her father could improve.

The danger Rachel faced was the possibility that, as she moved into that stage of life where she started looking for boyfriends, she could be drawn to insecure males like her father. She might then find herself working hard to reassure them or even earn their love. Of course, unless those young men faced their insecurity and worked to overcome it, that would be a losing proposition for Rachel.

What You Don't Know Can Hurt You

In my work with clients who are working to overcome Male Borderline Personality Disorder the conversation often turns to their children. Almost all of these men talk about strained relationships with their sons and daughters, and/or conflict with their wives over parenting. There is, I think, a good reason for this, and that is that men with MBPD have not had anything close to a functional upbringing. In a word, they don't know what a "normal" childhood or a healthy parent-child relationship should look like. No wonder they feel, as one father put it, "like the blind leading the blind" when it comes to parenting.

While it isn't possible to turn back the clock and have men with MBPD re-experience their formative years in a corrective way, what is possible is to provide these men with information and guidelines as to what their own children need from them, particularly in order to minimize the risk of repeating the pattern and promoting borderline traits and attitudes in the children they love.

The developmental needs of children are different from age to age. As our children move from infancy and toddlerhood to childhood, and then to adolescence, the challenges and critical tasks they face will change. As a consequence what they need most from us as parents, in order to successfully navigate those developmental passages, also changes.

What follows is useful information: Combined with some concrete guidelines and suggestions, fathers who are struggling to overcome MBPD, and who want to spare their sons and daughters the same fate, can use it to achieve that goal.

The social world our children are born into and must navigate successfully in order to reach a satisfying adulthood is anything but stress-free. In contrast to the "carefree childhood" that is the stuff of fantasies, childhood is actually fraught with challenges. If you doubt that, ask any eight or twelve year-old. For the man with BPD, though, having endured an upbringing marred by rejection or abandonment only makes the process of psychological survival that much more difficult. What I call effective parenting is parenting that is informed about children's needs at their different developmental levels, and stands ready to provide the kinds of support that will facilitate successful transitions from one stage to the next. Let's look at each of these developmental stages in turn.

INFANCY AND TODDLERHOOD: AGES ONE THROUGH FIVE

The most important developmental tasks facing children from

birth to about age five are the development of healthy attachments and exploration of the world around them, including the physical world and the social world. Children's first attachments are usually to their parents, but sometimes they become attached to one or more parental surrogates. The key here is that the adult(s) to whom the infant forms an attachment are able to reliably provide comfort and nurturance. Cuddling and feeding are the foundation for this. If that comfort and nurturance is unreliable, it communicates ambivalence at best toward the infant or child, and rejection or abandonment at worst.

While it was once a popular belief that mothers were infants' primary attachment figures, research has shown that fathers are equally important. The task for fathers in this scenario is simple: provide your infant and toddler with "comfort on demand." In other words, be ready to reach out with open arms when your child reaches out for you. Comfort him or her when he or she cries. Be reliable in this. In addition, be a parent who feeds your child, starting as soon as possible. Don't worry if you feel uncomfortable at first while trying this new behavior. Keep at it and in time you will find that not only does it get easier, but that it is actually as rewarding to you as it is to your child.

Fathers with MBPD may not have experienced much in the way of comforting and nurturance themselves, or it may have been very inconsistent; consequently, they may feel awkward being a source of comfort and nurturance to their own child. Think of it as the earliest way a human being can experience the acceptance we discussed earlier, and that turns out to play such an important role in personal security versus insecurity. It is the most fundamental way in which your child can feel accepted and loved by you.

Secure attachments, in turn, form the "base" from which the child ventures forth to explore the world. A securely attached child is free to learn and develop psychomotor and social competencies, including language.

When we are talking about young children's needs through these first crucial years, these two words should guide your actions as a parent: security and exploration. A securely attached child will venture forth and explore the world, and then eagerly return to you as his or her "base camp" for those explorations. He or she will get to know other young children and form the beginnings of relationships. Finally, he or she will be curious and brave.

As a father, you need to expect your infant and toddler child to look to you for cuddling on a regular basis. This reflects your child's most basic need for comfort and security (and acceptance) and you should expect this need to be heightened whenever your child feels anxious. During their earliest years men who go on to develop borderline traits may never have known this kind of "secure base." Accordingly, they may not know how to react when their son or daughter acts in a "clingy" way. My advice to them: Accept your child's need to cling and his or her need to turn to you for comfort and security.

AGES SIX TO ELEVEN

As children move from toddlerhood into later childhood—roughly ages six through eleven—the primary developmental challenges they face shift to socialization and literacy. To illustrate just how important this is, research has shown that children who are still struggling to read at the end of third grade are much less likely to finish high school than those who have mastered reading by then. Similarly, children who are "slow out of the gate" with respect to making friends by the time they are six or seven are vulnerable to being more or less social outcasts right through high school.

Literacy and socialization can be formidable challenges for many children. A few are fortunate to excel in both. Most, however, will struggle at times along the way. Fathers can play a vital role in helping their children navigate what can, at times, be treacherous waters. Fathers struggling to overcome MBPD, though, may not have memories of having been helped along the way with their own struggles. Many report that they were more or less left to fend for themselves—and act as if they expect their son or daughter to do the same. Some were even demeaned as a result of any academic or social struggles they may have experienced.

One complaint I have heard from many fathers (and mothers) is that it is difficult for them to understand much of the homework their children get. The reason for this is that teaching techniques are continuing to evolve at a fast pace. The result is that the way a parent was taught something as basic as arithmetic can be very different from the way their child is taught it—so much so that the parent feels at a loss to help. That's okay. Fathers need not go to school with their children in order to master the newest methods. Rather, here are a few ways that fathers can support their children's academic efforts:

- *Read Together.* This requires no special knowledge of educational methods. Beginning in first grade, take some time every day to read to, and later on to read with, your son or daughter. Correct them when they miss a word—but don't criticize them for it. If you are dealing with MBPD in your own life, a tendency to be overly self-critical can spill over into your relationship with your child. Keep an eye out for that tendency and avoid it as best you can. You will find that time spent reading together will not only help your child but will strengthen the bond between you.

- *Get Active in Your School.* The best schools are those in which there is measurable and consistent parental involvement. This includes attending regular conferences with teachers to review your child's academic progress and identify areas where there needs to be more work. However, involvement in your child's school also means going to social activities that are sponsored by the PTO/PTA, such as "ice cream socials" intended to encourage families to meet one another. It also means encouraging your child to partake in activities whether it's a school chorus or a "Lego Club" and then talking to him or her about those experiences.

• *Use the Internet*: Schools increasingly use the Internet to post homework assignments, and also to provide help to students (and parents) in understanding basic concepts and working through difficulties. Many teachers today also make themselves available via email.

YOUR CHILD'S EMERGING PERSONALITY

Parents almost always recognize some aspects of their child's unique "personality" starting in infancy. But it is during the years from six to ten that a child's personality and temperament really begin to stand out. It is during these years that you will begin to see just how outgoing versus shy, competitive versus noncompetitive, artistic, athletic, and so on that your son or daughter is. And this, too, can represent a challenge for the father whose upbringing resulted in his developing moderate or severe MBPD. The most common reason is that, as boys, these men were subject to *ambivalence* about who they were. Many report that they learned at an early age that it was okay for them to reveal only certain attitudes or behaviors. One man with MBPD, Dan, told me about how he had discovered that it was only okay to be aggressive:

> "I was a child who was interested in art. I liked drawing and could entertain myself for hours with a pencil and some paper. On the school bus I would draw every day. I was not

very aggressive, though, and so I tended to get teased and bullied. I remember that neither of my parents seemed very interested in my drawings, so I just kept them in a big box under my bed. One day, though, this bully punched me in the stomach and the nose after we'd gotten off the school bus and it had pulled away. I ran home holding my nose, and broke into tears as soon as I walked through the front door. My mother asked me what had happened and when I told her she asked me why hadn't punched back at the bully. I didn't know what to say so I just went to my room and did my homework.

"By suppertime my nose was swollen and red. My father looked at me from across the table and said something like "What happened to you?" My older brother said I'd gotten beat up on the school bus. I remember my father frowning as he turned to me. 'The next time you let yourself get beat up like that,' he said, I might just beat you up some more. No son of mine is going to be a wimp!'

"It was then and there that I decided I needed to get tough. I signed up for karate classes, worked my butt off, and ended up earning a black belt. To tell you the truth, though, I never once had to use any of that in self-defense. Maybe it was because everyone in school quickly found out that I was taking karate and doing really well. Or maybe it was that my attitude and behavior changed. I stopped drawing while riding on the school bus, and I think I just took on this mean expression. Anyway, no one bothered me again.

"I still enjoy drawing to this day, and I have even taken some painting classes. But that's not something I talk about much with my family."

It isn't difficult to imagine how Dan, as a father, could be tempted to repeat the pattern from his own upbringing with his own son, who had just turned six at the time we met. It was not that Dan was ambivalent at all about whether he loved his son. However, just as Dan had, the boy began to show a "soft" artistic side. He too liked to draw, and he was not particularly interested in competitive contact sports. Recalling his own early experiences, Dan worried that his son could become a victim of bullying. That, of course, is understandable. But what message would it have sent had this father chosen to discourage his son's interest, and even pressured him to drop art in favor of some competitive sport? While it might not have sown the seeds of full-blown MBPD in this boy (because Dan truly loved him), it could definitely have come across that Dad's love was conditional on what the son chose to pursue. Fortunately, that outcome was avoided by awareness and discussion between Dan and his therapist.

FAMILY TRADITIONS

Another important role that fathers can play during these childhood years is to establish and maintain family traditions. These traditions help to cement the bonds between family members. They include celebrating important holidays and birthdays; however, traditions can also be less complex (and more frequent) than that.

Fathers with MBPD often ask me for ideas about how they can strengthen the bond between them and their children, and I always suggest that they take the lead in establishing a couple of family traditions. Here are a few such traditions that emerged from our discussions (you may be able to think of more that you would enjoy with your family):

- Sunday barbecues during the summer months, with Dad doing the cooking (sometimes with some help).

- Friday night "pizza and a movie" night with the family picking out a movie to watch while feasting on pizza.

- Video game night. Dad sets aside an hour one night a week to roll up his sleeves and play video games.

- The monthly family outing. Dad asks for ideas and then picks one for a monthly Sunday outing. This may be a hike, a visit to a museum or other local attraction, or a meal out at a family restaurant.

Taking a child to Boy or Girl Scout meetings (or to other activities of the child's choice) are other ways of cementing the father-child relationship. One BPD father, for example, opted to carpool his ten-year-old daughter to her lacrosse matches. He'd either stay through the first half or get there in time to watch the second half, cheering along with the other parents. He found that this simple activity really strengthened the bond between him and his daughter.

Taking responsibility for one or more family traditions will build the bond between fathers and their children. It is another way to communicate to children that they are accepted and valued members of the family.

ADOLESCENCE: IDENTITY AND INDEPENDENCE

This developmental stage can be the most challenging of all for fathers with MBPD, for it represents that time in their children's lives when those children seek to carve out their individual identities and assert their independence. It is a difficult time for all parents, who often misinterpret their children's actions as rejection of them as parents. The title of a book on parenting teens—*Get Out of My Life, But First Could You Drive Me & Cheryl to the Mall?*—captures the essence of the dynamic that dominates this developmental stage.

The man with MBPD, as we know, is exquisitely sensitive to rejection. If that man also happens to be a father, maintaining relationships with his teen son or daughter can be that much more stressful. In this case the key is to keep in mind that teens actively seek out differences between themselves (and also siblings) in order to define who they are as individuals. This process is painful, as all of us who have passed through adolescence can attest. It is a period in our lives that is often romanticized, but for those who are living it, it can be anything but.

Adolescence is a time when we are acutely self-conscious, and also acutely conscious of our place on the social totem pole. We look for ways in which we can feel competent, unique, and attractive to others. We become aware of the options that are open to us (as well as options that are likely not open) for what our future will be. From the outside, teens love to put on a front of nonchalance—but on the inside there is nothing but turmoil.

Fathers with MBPD who are aware of the internal turmoil their teens are dealing with, as well as why it important for them to seek out differences in order to define who they are, may be better able to avoid feeling rejected or unappreciated when their sons and daughters enter adolescence. If there is any solace to be taken, it is that adolescence passes. Once a healthy identity is formed, the parent-child bond becomes even stronger.

SUMMING UP

As parents we are inclined to repeat the patterns of parenting we were exposed to as children— for better or worse. Clearly, men with MBPD experienced parenting that led in time to deep insecurity, self-hatred, free-floating anxiety, and all the other traits associated with MBPD. As fathers these men have a unique opportunity to break the pattern. To do so they must, first, be aware of their own MBPD and how it affects them. Second, by having a clear understanding of what their child really needs in terms of parenting as they grow up (as opposed to the parenting they received), they can assure that their own sons and daughters can be spared the struggle they have had to endure.